Jurassic Jackass: The Uffizi Museum of Dysfunction

By Francesca Vale

Copyright © 2025

All Rights Reserved

ISBN: 979-8-9938977-0-7

Dedication

To My Jurassic Jackass,

Thank you for your chaos, excuses, missed birthdays and scheduled appointments, unreturned housekeys, IKEA scheduling trauma, and many others. Without your emotionally frozen acrobatics, I'd have no museum, no comedic gold, and no book.

You are the star of the show.

Credit where *Dysfunction* is due.

Acknowledgements

To my rock, my anchor, and my lifelong partner in crime — Spuddy. For thirty-five years, you've been my reality check, cheerleader, and the first to grab popcorn when life turns into a telenovela. Thank you for always having my back, laughing at my stories and adventures, and for reminding me that survival is easier (and way more fun) with a BFF like you.

To the friends who supplied barriques of wine, Franciacorta, perspective, and sarcasm. To Martin, thank you for manning the emergency exits, offering live translation in the dialect of Dysfunctional Italian, and reminding me that "ciao" can mean hello, goodbye, or run for your life.

To my dog, Scarlett (aka Burrito), my loyal, unapologetically food-motivated dog and emotional support animal for this entire archaeological dig. You are missed, and the only creature in this book who regulated both of us successfully while I was writing this book.

The museum is still accepting new donations from the artist himself and from you, though the curator reserves the right to classify them under the "Extended Jurassic Jackass Dysfunction Series."

Since the museum is continually expanding, if you've encountered your own Jurassic Jackass, emotional velociraptor, or vintage specimen of avoidant behavior, consider this your invitation to submit your findings. Send your stories, artifacts, and field notes from the frontlines of dysfunction to the curator, because no museum is complete without visitor contributions.

Together, we can preserve these ancient behaviors for future generations… or at least laugh about them before extinction finally takes its course.

And ultimately, to every reader who's ever dated their own fossil—welcome. May this book save you the excavation.

Book Description

Jurassic Jackass: The Uffizi Museum of Dysfunction is a satirical memoir that turns heartbreak into high art. Told through a museum-style narrative of "exhibits," it curates one woman's relationship with a charmingly avoidant Italian man whose emotional architecture proves as unstable as a Renaissance ruin.

Francesca Vale, a real-estate writer and brand strategist, applies her eye for structure to the fragile frameworks of love and self-delusion. Each exhibit part essay, part confession uncovers the humor, absurdity, and strange beauty within emotional chaos. From *"Flat-Packed with Missing Screws," which captures the IKEA-grade assembly of modern relationships, to "The Archaeologist and the Ashes," a final excavation of lessons learned,* the book reframes dysfunction as an emotional anthropology.

With wit as sharp as a chisel and prose polished to a Renaissance shine, *Jurassic Jackass* is both brutally honest and unexpectedly tender and proves that even in the rubble of love gone wrong, there is still room for renovation.

About the Author

Francesca Vale is a professional real-estate writer, editor, and satirical memoirist whose work explores the architecture of human relationships with the same precision she once applied to luxury properties and market trends. A graduate of the Culinary Institute of America turned real estate professional, she spent two decades working across six cities—New York, Florence, Buenos Aires, Las Vegas, Denver, and beyond—before trading contracts and floor plans for character studies and emotional blueprints.

Drawing on her background in real estate, she views love, loss, and personal reinvention as structural projects: some beautifully designed, others held together by duct tape and denial. Her writing captures that intersection of heartbreak and humor—where chaos meets craftsmanship, and self-awareness becomes both a survival tool and a form of art.

Based in Florence, Italy, Francesca writes with one eye on human behavior and the other on the absurd contradictions of modern attachment. Her voice merges global perspective, psychological insight, and biting wit, inviting readers to laugh at the ruins and admire the renovation.

Her debut memoir, Jurassic Jackass: The Uffizi Museum of Dysfunction, curates emotional mayhem like a fine work of art. Told through a museum-style narrative of "exhibits," it chronicles her relationship with a charmingly avoidant Italian man—part love story, part field study in emotional anthropology. Beneath the satire lies a serious inquiry into how self-respect, humor, and boundaries can transform even the messiest heartbreak into something deeply instructive.

When she's not writing, Francesca lends her creative flair to real estate marketing and brand-storytelling projects—proving that even in the rubble of dysfunction, design still matters. She continues to split her time between Florence and her following creative excavation site, wherever that may be. Her passions include wining and dining, scuba diving, and advocating for animals.

Preface

I didn't set out to write a book. I set out to survive a love story that left me somewhere between Florence, IKEA, and a costly therapy bill.

What started as messages, field notes, and unsent emails turned into a museum of sorts, a collection of miscommunications, peak avoidant behavior, emotional fossils, ghosted birthdays, and a man who could meditate for 45 minutes but couldn't logically regulate for five.

This isn't a revenge book. It's an exhibit. You'll find satire, yes, but also grief, clarity, healing, and a few cracked candles from the gift shop.

Welcome to the Uffizi Museum of Dysfunction. May your exes never end up here, but if they do, at least you'll know where to put the plaque.

This is not any museum, but one built to house all the artifacts of a love story that burned bright, then collapsed under the weight of one man's inability to meet me on solid ground. Think of this book as a walking tour of that collapse, equal parts satire and soul excavation.

You'll find jokes. You'll find rage. You'll discover absurdity so sharp it draws blood. But underneath it all, you'll find a map. One that doesn't lead back to him, but back to me.

"I've watched hundreds of clients untangle from emotionally unavailable partners, but none have done it with the mix of incisive wit, self-awareness, and scorched-earth metaphor that Francesca brings to this museum of modern heartbreak. This is not

a story of victimhood, it's a blueprint of escape, preservation, and reclamation… all gift-wrapped in absurdity."

—Dr. Angela Delusioni, Museum Therapist-in-Residence.

Introduction

As most tragedies do, it began with promise and potential. What followed was a masterclass in avoidance so advanced that it deserved its own wing at the Uffizi Museum in Florence. Thus, the Jurassic Jackass Museum of Dysfunction was born, not out of love, but out of the sheer need to document the absurd and heal with humor.

For your own emotional safety, please keep your hands, hopes, and expectations away from the exhibits at all times. Welcome, dear visitor, to the Jurassic Jackass Museum of Dysfunction: a living archive dedicated to one man's spectacular collapse under the weight of his own emotional devolution, and to the woman who survived it with her humor intact.

What began as love, or at least a convincing impersonation of it, gradually disintegrated into a PhD study of avoidance, deflection, and emotional refrigeration. The exhibits you'll find here are not mere relics of heartbreak, but artifacts of absurdity: text messages preserved in their natural habitat of half-truths, fossilized promises, and glacial silences. Each one is a testament to the enduring mystery of how someone can be so intellectually awake yet so repressed.

This museum was not built out of bitterness, but out of a passion for anthropology. Every "we'll talk soon" and "vediamo" ("we'll see" in Italian) has been cataloged like pottery shards from a lost civilization, clues to the inner workings of the Jurassic Jackass, also known as JJ, a creature both tender and fascinating, yet infuriating, capable of empathy in theory and paralysis in practice.

And yet, buried beneath the rubble of ghosted plans and contradictory tenderness lies something almost noble: the proof that dysfunction can be art, provided you curate it well enough. So, wander freely. Admire the exhibits.

Take note of the missed pickup at the train station in Santa Maria Novella, the Gaslight Noir candle collection flickering inconsistently in our gift shop, and the limited-run Therapy Reminder ringtone playing softly in the distance.

Somewhere between the Birthday Fiasco (featuring random pool photos), the flagship key retrieval epic, the ghost dog memorial, the IKEA Edition (Assembly Required, Emotional Regulation Not Included), and the dozen handwritten letters valiantly hurled at the Jurassic skull of JJ, you'll find proof that chaos, when well documented, becomes its own form of modern art.

Above all, remember this: what you see here is not tragedy, it's taxonomy. Every heartbreak deserves to evolve into humor, and every fossilized feeling deserves a proper display case.

The star of our show was offered a sneak peek at some of his own exhibits. As the curator, I handed him a glitter bomb of self-awareness: a full-color tour through his own dysfunction turned into literary art. He responded as if he were signing for a DHL package.

He replied with the enthusiasm of a man reading IKEA instructions upside down, in Swedish hieroglyphs. Just two words: "Ok, grazie." This gave birth to our popular *Ok Grazie* tote, available at the gift shop, a timeless tribute to emotional minimalism and the art of doing the absolute least.

True to form, the artist then vanished into his natural habitat of silence, the emotional equivalent of a tumbleweed rolling through the Museum of Accountability.

Welcome to the Jurassic Jackass Uffizi Museum of Dysfunction.

Exhibit 1: The Garden After Dark: Where the Avoidant Flora Blooms

Even the most beautiful gardens have shadows.

After two and a half months, the pattern I first saw in January had matured into a whole ecosystem, leaving me slightly confused.

He would often retreat into himself without warning, vanish behind polite excuses, and reappear as if nothing had happened. He used "Ciao, com'è stai?" the way most people use a fire extinguisher, break glass in case of emotional damage. But instead of putting out fires, it was meant to erase them fantastically.

It was his signature move, up until I burned it to the ground. It was a spiritual bypass disguised as small talk. He treated it like the emotional equivalent of unplugging the Wi-Fi router: if I restart this conversation, maybe the last crash didn't happen.

I remember the crash. I cataloged the collision for you to learn, laugh, and enjoy.

I refuse to let the museum burn down because it is ready for another tour.

He thinks "Ciao, com'è stai?" is a gentle check-in. I know it is just the next track on his Fossilized Avoidant Playlist™, right between *Selective Amnesia (Acoustic Version)* and *I Thought We Were Fine (Live from Denial Stadium)*.

Each time, I forgave the disconnection. Perhaps it was he evaluating the relationship. But I sensed fear and a lack of knowing how to repair.

What I did not know then was that I was falling in love with a man who had already learned how to disappear, not from me, but from himself.

The laughter continued, but it came with an undercurrent I could not name. The same man who once held me so close was already slipping through my fingers, one silence at a time. Luckily, I quickly realized there was a serious issue, and by the fifth month, he was in therapy.

With all the travel I was doing, hopping continents, airports, and existential crises, JJ and I realistically spent about two and a half months together in total. Yet somehow, that was plenty of time for the dysfunction to start wafting through like an overripe Camembert left out baking in the summer sun. I smelled it right on schedule, as if avoidance issues have an expiration date.

I am not a fragile traveler looking for rescue. I have lived all over the world on what I like to call solo excavations, digging through new cultures, strange apartments, and, at times, my own emotional rubble. No shortcuts, no "journey" hashtags.

I once told JJ, "Each soft edge you admire was once a sharp corner, worn down by heartbreak, by betrayal, by the aching labor of healing. Kindness was forged from moments when cruelty would have been easier."

He nodded thoughtfully, as if I had handed him a user manual he would never read.

"The sweetness you taste is a choice I made after bitterness tried to claim me. My sensitivity, it is attunement, learned from surviving in places where silence screamed louder than words. And that depth? That is what happens when you drown and learn how to breathe underwater."

In short, a well-seasoned archaeological site of emotional resilience, fully excavated, cataloged, and open for guided tours. At that very time, my Jurassic Jackass was still busy drawing a treasure map to his own empathy, somewhere between denial and defensive sarcasm.

And, it's when he is away from me that his demons throw a house party. And boy, what a party.

We are talking a full-blown rager in his psyche, lights flashing, Self-Doubt doing shots off the kitchen counter, Avoidance grinding on Insecurity in the corner while Anxiety DJs from the playlist titled "Women Who Cared Too Much."

The host, of course, is Denial, wearing Jurassic Jackass's favorite blazer and insisting everything is fine. Meanwhile, Empathy got an invite but did not show up, as usual. She texted, "Sorry, not feeling it tonight," and ghosted.

By midnight, Projection has broken a lamp, Overthinking is sobbing in the bathroom, and Guilt is outside smoking, saying, "She deserves better, but what can I do?"

It is chaos in there; a complete mental mosh pit. When I think the music is dying down, Self-Sabotage decides it is the perfect time for karaoke. The song? "Don't Speak."

The next morning, JJ wakes up emotionally hungover, wondering why everything feels off, like the ghosts of bad decisions past have possessed him. But do not worry, he will text me something thoughtful like "Ciao, com'è stai?" three days later, like clockwork, as if his entire subconscious did not trash the place while I was gone.

On a more serious note, according to attachment theory, this is not unusual for someone with avoidant tendencies. Emotional safety in proximity can create a temporary sense of regulation, but once the source of that safety leaves, the nervous system reboots into survival mode.

His body knows I am safe, his brain, however, is still running Windows 1998: slow to update and prone to crashing.

Research on co-regulation shows that compassionate, attuned relationships can help soothe even the most anxious systems. Still, without the ability to self-regulate, he becomes a walking glitch the moment I am out of range.

The problem is getting him to the table.

Exhibit 2: The Garden of Ghostly Delights

Where red flags masquerade as roses.

It began the way the best stories do, not with fireworks, but with laughter. The easy kind that pulls you in before you realize you are already attached. From the start, the chemistry was undeniable: a magnetic pull, shared glances that lingered too long, the feeling of having met someone you had somehow always known.

When he forgot his scarf at my flat, he remarked, "I need to keep finding a reason to come back here to see you." My reply was that he did not need a reason. He followed up with, "I want you in my life forever."

Then, as suddenly as it began, he disappeared.

As I think back, I mentioned during pillow talk, mind you, that my "brother" from Rome might be coming for the weekend, and that I wanted him to meet him. He said, "Forse." "Magari." My response was, "Seriously?" I thought he was joking, but he was not.

This was my first red flag of confusion, probably two weeks into seeing each other, and after about five nights spent overnight. People who mean a lot to you, and whom you mean a lot to, are usually delighted to be introduced and to meet their inner circle of friends and family.

It had been about thirteen or fourteen years since my last serious relationship, because I had never found anyone suitable whom I truly liked. He seemed like he was in, so in fairness, I felt I had to give it a shot as well.

I remember thinking, in the beginning, that he needed to slow down. The chemistry was like being hit by a freight train wrapped in poetry, intoxicating, cinematic, and far too much for someone who wanted to enjoy her wine without emotional whiplash.

I found it strange, not alarming, just confusing, like opening the fridge and finding your car keys inside.

Then came Red Flag Number Two: the legendary "flu." Partly true, but for the most part, metaphorical.

He vanished for about a month, citing illness. When someone is sick, food is often the last thing they want to deal with, so I offered to bring him soup twice. Homemade, not supermarket grade. Not even a "thanks, but no." Just no response. Perhaps he was embarrassed to be seen sick. Maybe he was feverish and pale, wrapped in the blankets of masculine pride. What I did not realize was that this was the dress rehearsal for the main event, his vanishing act series, Volume I of what would later become a common denominator across all the exhibits in the Museum of Dysfunction.

A month later, he turned up at an event, cured, and asked me if we could finally be intimate. For a few weeks, the world was bright again, or I was dazzled by denial's spotlight.

Then came Red Flag Number Three: the breakup text. Delivered with all the emotional warmth of a system update. He said he had gotten out of a two-year relationship the previous October. It was now March. We had started our little dance in January, with that convenient one-month flu intermission.

Evidently, this was his idea of pacing himself: one month of intensity, one month of hibernation, followed by an existential exit when I dared to ask him to commit to, wait for it, an event.

The pattern was forming, and the Museum was already taking shape.

Carissima Francesca,

Sweetheart, you wrote some excellent and moving words, as no one has ever written to me before.

I'm sorry to have caused you pain, and I have caused pain to myself, too. The pain would have been much greater later.

You have understood everything about me, intuiting it with your sensitivity.

What I felt and feel with you was sincere and excellent, and I thank God for making me meet you, beautiful and sensitive, and for the wonderful moments spent together, so profound and engaging and, at the same time, so funny. I never thought I could laugh so much and share so much in such a short time. There are people who do not live what we have experienced together in an entire lifetime. I am also deeply saddened to have interrupted our beautiful idyll, but I felt that I was not yet ready, and that if I had continued in those conditions, I would have disrespected you and done you serious wrong.

I love you very much. You are adorable. I felt very loved, understood, and desired, never used. I felt safe, and I hope I made you feel the same. I hope you understood and felt the same, because I wanted to give the same thing to you: to trust you and to be able to trust me. For this reason, when I felt that I was not yet quite ready, I had to find the courage to interrupt our love. It cost me so much, because we were so good together and I was happy. Leaving a wonderful garden to head alone toward a desert, without knowing or having any idea where to go, is not easy.

By now, I have almost gotten used to loneliness, but it is not a condition I like. My biggest dream was, and is, to have a family and feel the warmth of mutual love and deep sharing. I must say that with you, I felt all this, and great joy.

We are very similar in many ways, starting with the conflictual relationship with a somewhat self-centered and manipulative father who influenced our life choices, and leading to the necessary and consequent desire for freedom and detachment. I would have a lot to say about the damage parents inflict on their children. Some manage to overcome it, and others struggle more. Perhaps this is also why I did not have a family and did not have children. It is for this reason that sometimes my loneliness wins over my desire to live and share. And having had a meaningful relationship that ended a short time ago, one of the few in which I had really hoped to stop, to get married, to have a family, and to which I dedicated all of myself, only to be deeply disappointed, I still did not feel completely free psychologically, even if I have an infinite need to give and receive love. Thank you because I felt loved, and I loved you.

I'm very confused, but when you love someone and decide to live together, you have to be sure and have a light soul to be able to give joy and happiness to the other. Right now, I am not yet fully able to do that. But of course, I know that it was very nice to be together with you.

Your soul is beautiful, sensitive, delicate. I perceived it. I saw your eyes in the depths, your lovely smile, your gaze so sweet and so true. We also spoke with our eyes, and those, too, were caresses.

I want to write much more, but I would never finish. I want you to receive this message because I would have liked to share it with you earlier, but it is difficult for me to open my heart and speak and write so openly, even though I have always done so with you. I didn't want to let you down. I didn't want to hurt you.

Darling, I am there for you, and I will always be there, because two souls who meet as ours met are rare and precious.

I love you, and I kiss you,

JJ

It broke my heart, but I respected it, and I went silent. Then, after a week, Florence, ever the meddler, put us in the same room again. The moment our eyes met, it was over. Our arms naturally moved into an unconscious embrace, and the entire crowded room of that party no longer existed. The rest of the night was spent in each other's arms, tucked into secluded little spots around the venue. He told me how happy he was, how being with me made him feel alive again. During dinner that evening, I was embarrassed by his openness and affection in front of two strangers, as well as his public displays of affection at the dinner table. After that, it felt like we were finding our way back to something real. We both got STD tested so we could be exclusive.

Exhibit 3: The Man I Miss
Where the armor slips, and something real shows through.

Most visitors expect the noise, the volatility, the evasive maneuvers worthy of a seasoned escape artist. What they do not expect is this: a small collection of soft, human moments that complicate the entire narrative.

There were nights when we would stay up talking until four or five in the morning, sharing stories, laughing until we were both delirious and glowing.

There was one dinner where his joy slipped out in public. We exchanged a private joke, nothing elaborate, just something only the two of us understood, and he exploded into laughter so loud, so unfiltered, so wildly uncharacteristic of his carefully curated Florentine cool, that Martin stopped mid-fork, staring at him as if he had witnessed a rare cosmic event.

I explained to Martin, "This is what JJ and I do late at night after we get home from going out." A simple truth: the dinosaur could roar with joy when he forgot he was supposed to be composed.

Another time, at another dinner, we were not even sitting directly across from each other, just diagonally, with a table full of people between us. I scooted down ever so slightly, stretched out my leg far enough under the table, and rubbed his leg with my foot. He looked genuinely confused, as if a polite ghost was haunting him.

Then he followed the invisible thread back to my eyes. I smiled, and we both laughed.

He smiled, that smile, the stifled, boyish, caught-off-guard grin that has to be the cutest thing you ever saw on him. A tiny spark of mischief he did not show the world, but always showed me.

What this does is remind the visitor that dysfunction is rarely one-note. JJ's sweetness was not consistent; it was not enough; it was not sustainable.

But it was real.

And perhaps that is why it lives here, behind glass, under soft museum lighting: not to romanticize him, not to resurrect anything, but to acknowledge the truth.

That even my Jurassic Jackass has a heart.

Exhibit 4: The Birth of Jurassic Jackass

The Exhibit That Bit Back.

At first, he seemed like the archetypal sophisticated Florentine man, articulate, attentive, sensitive, perceptive in that poetic Pisces way that could make anyone believe in cosmic compatibility.

The man I once believed had depth revealed himself to be a limited-edition, bespoke, ultra-luxury model of emotional dysfunction, handcrafted somewhere between denial and delusion, with custom inlays of self-sabotage.

From what I can tell, I was "special." Apparently, I did not just meet his surface self; I activated the nuclear level of his dysfunction.

I have always loved dinosaurs. Something is thrilling about creatures that are ancient, majestic, and incapable of coexisting peacefully in a domestic environment. I used to joke that I wanted a pet Velociraptor like Blue from Jurassic World: Dominion (2022): intelligent, loyal, misunderstood, but also unpredictable, feral, and a little bit deadly.

Well, the universe listened. And, as it often does, it delivered what I asked for, in human form.

A creature who could be tender one moment and vanish into the trampled ferns the next. You could feed him trust, care, and consistency, but the moment he caught the scent of vulnerability, he would dart for the hills, leaving only footprints, chaos, and confusion behind.

He was not my boyfriend. He was my behavioral research project. My private exhibit. My PhD in psychology.

And the more I studied him, the clearer it became: I had not fallen in love with a man. I had adopted a Jurassic-era emotional rescue case, complete with claws, charm, and a permanent freeze response.

Exhibit 5: The Velociraptor and Wreckage: Enrollments, Accidents & Obedience School

Lessons in Boundaries, Bite Marks, and Behavioral Reform.

He was like an untrained puppy I let into my home, except the house was my heart.

At first, it felt sweet. Endearing. A little chaotic, yes, but is that not how love sometimes starts? A few knocks, some nerves, the clumsy excitement of something new. I thought that if I gave it time, patience, and warmth, he would settle.

He would learn what not to chew, where to do his business, and how not to knock over every carefully placed boundary I had built with my bare hands.

But instead, he tore through the place like a velociraptor. He gnawed through the furniture of my trust, leaving messes in places I did not know I had left open. He knocked over the things I kept sacred, my peace, my time, my dignity, and then looked up at me with wide, clueless eyes, a big, destructive tail wagging, as if to say, "Wait... was that not okay?" Except his equivalent was "Ciao, com'è stai?"

And the worst part? I still tried to offer him a treat on the way out. I still tried to coax him back, hoping this time he would come in soft, stay present, and learn to curl up safely by the hearth of my affection.

The mess was part of the magic, like getting a brand-new puppy.

But soon the furniture was chewed to a pulp, the floor stained, the curtains torn from their rods. My peace unraveled thread by thread, pulled loose by the teeth of someone who did not know how to exist without causing damage, and did not seem all that interested in learning. That is when I knew I needed professional help.

Exhibit 6: Lead Paleontologist: Excavator of Feelings Buried Under 40,000 Years of Avoidance

Specializing in softening fossils and dodging emotional tail-whips.

Being the only caretaker who formed a real bond with him, not the curated version he trotted out for public charm, but the one he hid from himself, I found myself in unfamiliar territory. As his museum curator and paddock handler, unlike his predecessors, I spoke his language and had a high level of emotional fluency with him. It took me a while to understand what was happening.

I mentioned that we could speak about the relationship again in a few months. No rush, I was more interested in building intimacy and trust than rushing into a relationship.

But the deeper we went, the colder he became. He did not disappear; he was steadily calcifying out of fear.

One moment, we were cruising toward a future full of connection and shared vision; the next, I was trying to locate his empathy on Google Maps and getting a 404 error.

That is when the doubt started creeping in. No doubt in him, oddly enough, because we never doubted the love we had for each other, not for a nanosecond, but doubt in myself.

I had always trusted my intuition, yet I found myself second-guessing and confused. I hadn't thought about the original avoidant in decades. Not once. Not until I moved into my second flat in Florence did I place a ceramic chicken on the terrace table that came with the apartment. I named it Eric without thinking — a private joke, really

— because his name in French translates to rooster. It felt harmless. Decorative.

And then one day, without warning, it clicked.

The feeling.

That low-grade unease. The polite distance. The warmth that never quite landed. It was the same atmospheric pressure I'd lived under all those years ago — the same sensation of reaching for something that quietly withdrew. I hadn't remembered the man. My body had remembered the pattern. It was an eerie, faintly familiar feeling I had experienced before. I could not place it. Then one day, it all came together. Not the exact fossil, but indeed the skeletal remains of the same emotional species.

Back then, I did not bother to get to the bottom of it. I moved on.

This time, my gut knew something was off, but I did not know what to call it. So, I did what any normal person with a spiraling hunch and an internet connection would do: I went digging and not Googling. Excavating.

I knew that every time things became intimate, JJ would vanish like a magician pulling a disappearing act with feelings instead of rabbits.

This time, I was faced with another avoidant, only with better hair and more artisanal excuses. But this time, I was not as confused as before. I recognized the twitchy silence, the emotional buffering, the moment panic would set in whenever I said something involving feelings, plans, or accountability.

And I thought: I know this fossil. I have carbon-dated this behavior before. Now, I had tools. Emotional taxonomy. A psychological trowel and decades of experience.

So, I grabbed my metaphorical brush, threw on my khakis, and got to work. This was not just a man; this was an entire avoidant species, and I had the chance to study it up close. So, I did what I always do when something does not add up: I dug for hours.

What began as a search to understand one internally frozen Florentine man turned into a full-blown paleontological dig through the strata of every relationship I had ever had. And there, buried beneath years of well-masked dysfunction, I found the pattern:

The Flight.
The Freeze.
The Fossil.

And thus began the founding of this project, not to document Florentine men like their architecture — gorgeous, historic, and wholly frozen in time.

But when you enter this UNESCO heritage site, there are no emotional renovations allowed, and certainly no modern plumbing for feelings, only a mandate to honor the long line of emotionally paralyzed ancestors who came before him. Built for display, not for emotional occupancy.

Some people collect red flags. I collect bones.

After a while, the words appeared, blinking at me like a diagnosis: Avoidant. Emotional paralysis. Everything clicked into place.

The cycles of approach and withdrawal, connection and confusion, were not random. They were learned survival tactics, deeply ingrained.

I was not imagining the shift. I had wandered into a part of him no one else had ever reached, and it terrified him.

I had slipped past his natural defense system, the one built over the years to guard the parts of himself he did not want seen, let alone loved. Most people only encountered the curated version: charming, clever, intermittently present, and mysterious.

I got behind the display glass. Not because I forced my way in, but because I spoke his language: emotional fluency, nervous-system literacy, the ability to sense the tremors beneath his stillness.

That is why, when I asked him if he had ever behaved like this in past relationships, he said no because he had not. Not like this. Not at this level.

But this was not new. It was not born overnight. What he offered others was the basic model, charming, aloof, manageable.

The care I had for him offered depth, not drama; intimacy, not performance; and a home, not a hiding place. That depth terrified him. The dinosaur froze in permafrost as the relationship deepened.

Not out of cruelty. Out of overwhelm. It was not because I was too much. It was because I was the first person who made him feel everything he had spent years avoiding.

One minute, we were discussing dreams and spirituality; the next, I was negotiating emotional landmines he swore weren't there.

That was the day the Museum began, not out of bitterness but out of clarity. That was the moment I stopped asking, "Why is he like this?" and started labeling display cases.

Exhibit 7: The Juliet Balcony of Emotional Freefall

Where Gravity Worked, But Empathy Did Not.

I was staying in my first Florence palazzo, complete with a Juliet balcony that makes you feel like you are starring in your own romantic film, until, of course, your prop glass of wine goes rogue, swan-dives onto the street below, and explodes into smithereens.

No one was hurt, thank God, but my heart was racing. I had just come back from a trip, still half-packed, half-alive, and thought: this is what relationships are for, right? In a moment of crisis, you call your person, and they show up.

So, I called JJ. He answered, shockingly. His opening line: "Do you need the name of an attorney?"

Ah, yes, because what every trembling woman needs after nearly committing accidental manslaughter with a Chianti glass is legal counsel, not comfort.

I texted that I was scared and jittery, said I felt alone, and asked him to come over. Cue the rustling of leaves, the sound of my emotional raptor disappearing into the brush.

He never showed up. No follow-up, no "are you okay," not even a carrier pigeon of concern. Just the digital tumbleweed of silence rolling through my WhatsApp chat.

So, I cleaned up the mess myself, poured another glass (indoors this time), and toasted to self-sufficiency, the house wine of women who date emotionally unavailable men. But the balcony was not done with me yet. A day or two later, I noticed my potted plant had fallen too and was hanging off the ledge like a suicidal geranium. I texted again, thinking this time he would redeem himself with a small act of heroism.

His response: "Is it dangerous?"

Not "I'll be right there."
Not "Want me to come help?"

Just pure, distilled JJ logic, a one-person symposium on how to underperform empathy in any situation.

Gravity: reliable.
Jurassic Jackass: less so.

Exhibit 8: The Hoxton Soft-Opening and the Hard-Closing of My Patience

3 March: Early Warning Signs, Ignored in Candlelight.

Three weeks into dating Jurassic Jackass, we had our first social test: dinner at the Hoxton Hotel soft opening, hosted by my friend Martin. It was supposed to be a simple yes-or-no RSVP. Instead, it became an archaeological dig through layers of non-commitment.

Martin asked me to confirm whether JJ was coming. I asked JJ. He gave me a reply that could best be described as linguistic Jell-O, shaky, translucent, and offering zero structure. For three days, I prodded, texted, and clarified, trying to extract a sentence containing both a verb and a plan.

By the morning of the event, Martin pinged me again: "So… is he coming? Because he was unclear."
My answer: "I have no idea. He's being non-committal with me, too. He's your problem now."

I had to hand the fossil over like a cursed artifact. "Good luck, Professor."

Martin admitted later, "With Italians, it's always an uphill battle." I thought he meant charming lateness or double-booked aperitivos. Little did I know I was signing up for the emotional equivalent of the Tour de Chaos, complete with missing gears, no brakes, and a rider who sometimes pretends the finish line does not exist.

JJ did show up. He picked me up by cab, but I said, "Let's walk since it is only three blocks away," and that it would be a nice opportunity to spend more time together in private. The man thrives on last-minute entrances and cinematic tension. I was happy to see him; optimism is a hell of a drug.

But that night should have been a museum-grade clue: if confirming dinner required a small task force, imagine what scheduling therapy, IKEA, or accountability would look like. The Hoxton dinner was billed as a soft opening, but in retrospect, it was really the grand opening of red flags, complete with prosecco, polished lighting, and a preview of the endurance sport that dating him would become.

Over time, this evolved into a full-blown pattern. I would be halfway into pajamas, serum applied, hair in a towel, when I would get "Ciao, vuoi venire a cena?" at 9:47 p.m. on a Tuesday.

At first, I tried to be spontaneous. I told myself, "Maybe this is the Italian way, la dolce vita, unplanned joy!" But after the fifteenth episode of *Guess Who's Texting at the Eleventh Hour?*, I realized it was not the dolce vita. It was dysfunctional scheduling dressed as romance. After too many nights of half-blow-dried chaos, I finally said, "Okay, it's been fun, but I cannot live like this. You need to respect my schedule, too."

Martin started calling him "The Midnight Cowboy," not because he owned a hat, but because every invitation, apology, or half-baked plan arrived somewhere between 11:00 p.m. and the next bad decision.

It became his brand: galloping in at the last possible minute with a casual "Ciao, ci sei?" while everyone else was already ordering dessert or halfway to bed. Somewhere in the Museum of Dysfunction, there is an empty chair at every dinner table, reserved in his honor, a permanent installation titled *He's On His Way*.

Because even spontaneous Italians have a bedtime, and this curator has a skincare routine. At that point, I considered adding a sign to my front door that read: Miracles Accepted Until 8:00 p.m. After That, It's Pajama Theology.

Exhibit 9: Ghosted at Gate 4

He said he'd be there. So did my dignity. Neither showed up.

It started like a postcard: Hurghada, Egypt, spring break, a plan with Cristiano (my honorary non-blood brother of thirty-plus years from Rome) to escape the Florence chaos and spend a few lazy days somewhere warm. Egypt sounded perfect: sunshine, coral reefs, and, ideally, a functioning boyfriend.

But when it came time to plan the trip, my dear Velociraptor (not yet full JJ mode) froze like an Excel sheet mid-update. Questions such as "Is this budget okay for you?" suddenly became as complex as quantum physics. He did, however, manage to solve the riddle in true JJ fashion, with a breakup text. Because why communicate when you can detonate?

So, I pivoted. If I were going to be alone at a resort, I might as well go all in on solitude. I booked a ten-day Red Sea live-aboard dive trip to Hurghada, figuring salt water might disinfect whatever emotional wound he had reopened. Somewhere between the booking and the boarding, we made up, because dysfunction, much like bad Wi-Fi, always reconnects.

Then came the Café Paszkowski moment. Piazza della Repubblica, late at night. He asked actual human questions: When are you leaving? Who are you going with? How long will you be gone? And I, naïvely, mistook this for progress. He rested his head on my shoulder and held my hand in a crowded café, like a man practicing for an intimacy exam he had decided to pass. I thought to myself: *Aha, a breakthrough.*

Spoiler alert: he was circling a cul-de-sac.

Within seventy-two hours, he vanished again, classic "ghosting with espresso intervals." By then, I had learned to anticipate these absences the way one anticipates long weekends: plan social outings, schedule distractions, and wait for the inevitable reset text, "Ciao, com'è stai?"

When the trip day finally arrived, he briefly redeemed himself with a cinematic goodbye: cab fare paid, luggage loaded, kisses at the bus door, and accompaniment to Piazza della Indipendenza for dog-sitter drop-off. He promised to pick me up when I returned from Milan. For twenty-four hours, I genuinely believed I was dating a grown man.

On board the vessel, we had cell phone signal for the first two to three days, then none for four days. When our dive boat finally regained signal, my phone showed zero messages from him. Not even a "Buon immersione." I texted him cheerful updates anyway, because that is what functional people do.

His reply?

He was "working a lot" and had decided to take "a last-minute holiday."

Translation: not only would he not pick me up, but he also wanted me to know he was relaxing while I hauled dive gear and broken promises through the chaos of Stazione di Santa Maria Novella. By then, I had stopped counting the broken promises: fish restaurants that never existed, bars in Forte dei Marmi we never saw, weekend trips to Rome, "next weekends" that dissolved faster than sea foam.

I learned the only thing more unreliable than an Italian train schedule is Jurassic Jackass's follow-through.

Exhibit 10: The Cantinetta Mirage (A Study in Romantic Food Poisoning)

Featuring a Guest Appearance by a Securely Attached Shark, The Only Male Who Showed Up When I Needed Him.

Sitting in my live-aboard cabin, somewhere between nausea and enlightenment, I felt somatically ill at the thought of him. The sea was calm, but my stomach was staging a coup. I kept thinking: *Who is this man?*

Flashback to Florence: Cantinetta delle Terme, my favorite seafood sanctuary, the kind of place where the plates are art, and the wine list could qualify for sainthood.

I dropped off my furs at Bellagambi before dinner (because even my winter wardrobe needs therapy) and made sure to handle the dinner reservation myself before heading to his flat. I was not about to let the logistics fall victim to his signature "organizational blackout." And there he was all evening, charming, attentive, carrying my giant tote bag like a receptive and available sherpa.

The evening was perfect, at his place and at the restaurant. Rooftop terrace laughter at his home, confessions under Tuscan moonlight, easy conversation, and that deceptive warmth that makes you think, *this time the velociraptor evolved thumbs*. I looked at him and thought, *He's trying*.

Cut to now: I was on a dive boat, clutching my stomach, scrolling through photos of that night like crime scene evidence. He was as recognizable to me as a witness-protection headshot.

The body remembers, though, the laughter, the ease, and that is what made it worse. I spent the next three days performing a complete spiritual exorcism: deleting messages, breathing exercises, silent mantras like *I will not text the fossil.*

By day three, I had almost expelled him from my system, though if emotional toxicity burned calories, I would be in supermodel territory by now.

And just when I thought the universe had finished mocking me, a longimanus, an actual oceanic whitetip shark, appeared at the end of our dive. He made a cinematic, last-minute entrance, was offered a friendly boop on the nose, radiated unabashed main-character energy, and demonstrated a level of secure attachment rarely found on land.

Imagine that: a literal apex predator with prehistoric instincts was less avoidant than JJ. A shark with dead black eyes and a bite radius large enough to end my memoir swam calmly toward me with more emotional consistency than a grown Italian man who panics when asked about dinner plans.

As he drifted toward the group, unbothered and beautifully present, it hit me with embarrassing clarity: this shark understands intimacy better than he does. At least the longimanus shows up when he senses a connection; JJ flees as if he had smelled a gas leak.

Somewhere between the nausea, the shark encounter, and the three-day spiritual detox, the truth finally crystallized. Cantinetta delle Terme was not the problem. The seafood was not the problem. My stomach was not the problem.

And sometimes it takes a bout of romantic food poisoning, followed by a near-religious encounter with a well-adjusted shark, to see a man clearly.

Exhibit 11: Saltwater & Second Chances (God Help Me)

Because Apparently, I Needed One More Field Trip in Dysfunction.

After the dive trip, I emerged from the emotional deep end pruned, pissed, and spiritually pickled. I wanted nothing to do with him. I went full witness-protection mode, no sightings, no emotional contraband, for five solid weeks. He kept trying, of course. Little messages floated in like carrier pigeons of denial: "Ciao, com'è stai?" "Hope you are refreshed from your vacation." "Let's meet." I ignored every one of them like spam calls from the universe.

Then came the beach invitation. Out of nowhere, Captain Avoidance decided to swap incense for sunscreen. "Let's go to the sea," he said, like Poseidon offering therapy. I should have said no, but curiosity is my most persistent toxic trait. This was not the usual twilight circus of dinner, events, wine, and repressed emotion. This was daytime. Open air. UV exposure. A full day with the man who could barely manage an hour of emotional clarity indoors.

I thought maybe daylight would do what moonlight could not: reveal the man behind the mirage. Or at least show me whether he sparkles or burns when hit with direct sunlight. Either way, I packed SPF 50, emotional armor, and the faint hope that the Jurassic Jackass might evolve gills for self-awareness.

He kept texting, trying to see me. I kept declining until he dangled a Forte dei Marmi day trip like some emotionally haunted bait.

Forte dei Marmi was the first time I ever saw JJ in water, actual water, not the metaphorical emotional kind he spends his life avoiding like a medieval plague. And, as with everything with him, even swimming became a psychological case study.

There he was: six feet two inches of Florentine Jurassic Jackass standing at the shoreline, as if the Tyrrhenian Sea had personally offended him. He scanned the horizon the same way he scans relationships, calculating depth, distance, and all possible escape routes.

When he finally walked in, he did not swim; he paddled in that stiff, determined way that looks almost athletic from afar but up close is just pure avoidant panic wearing sunglasses. I realized in that moment that a JJ in water is a whole separate species, *Homo Avoidanticus Aquaticus*, equipped with the JJ Paddle™: powerful kicks, zero arm involvement, because he refuses to use the parts of himself that would actually help.

There was selective buoyancy, where he floated better whenever I was nearby, which is basically the entire relationship dynamic in one marine metaphor.

There were silent drowning vibes; he would rather sink to the ocean floor than admit he was overwhelmed.

There was directional obsession: swimming only parallel to the shore, never toward me unless I turned away—classic aquatic push-pull.

Watching him splash around in the bluest water Italy has to offer, I had the strangest thought: this man could survive a prehistoric ocean, but not a straightforward question about his feelings. Evolution is wild.

I knew something was off the moment I got in the car. He was squirrelly, fidgety, snapping at drivers, short-fused, and unglued from his usual slow-motion Pisces calm. I kept things light until I found a good entry point on the way back to Florence, with a captive audience, in the middle of traffic, to bring up the whole "forgot to show up at the train station when you promised" situation.

I was not hostile. I was clinical. Because at this point, we were not dealing with a misunderstanding; we were dealing with character.

You do not get to vanish at the last minute for a vacation and act like the problem was logistics. I told him this would be the first and last time we would talk about it, not because it did not matter, but because I refused to nag a grown man like a toddler.

A real adult owns his missteps. A real adult apologizes without being cornered in highway traffic. I got one: a weak, whispery "I'm sorry." I only caught it because I was watching his mouth move, just the bare minimum amount of air required to qualify as remorse, technically.

On the way back to the city, he got a last-minute call about a party and asked if I wanted to come. I had hoped we would spend the evening alone. But of course, I said yes. And because this is Florence, where "normal" includes hosting dinner with men who emotionally vanish, and then hand you a tote bag full of olives as if that balances the scale.

At the party, he carried my Gucci tote and introduced me around, then disappeared into the crowd. No problem, I do not need a handler. What I did not appreciate was the post-party follow-up from one of his friends.

Let's call him Chef Flirtolini.

He texted me the next day, casual at first. Then came: "I hope I dream of you." And: "You know I wanted to kiss you the night of the party." I thought, *Oh, did you? While I was sitting on JJ's lap, no less?*

Chef Flirtolini had the nerve to invite us, yes, *us*, to a party at his house the following weekend, but amazingly, "forgot" to invite JJ in the actual follow-up message—just me.

He offered to pick me up at the train station and help him cook and set up, as if I had agreed to do free labor for a man I hardly knew who tried to flirt me into his kitchen. I told him I would be riding with JJ. Boundaries. Respect. Manners. Concepts apparently foreign to both him and JJ.

When I brought it up to JJ, I said, "You need to deal with your friends grazing on me. I'm not out here in an open field wearing a 'free samples' sign."

But this would not be the first time.

Exhibit 12: The Grazer 2: Return of the Free-Range Avoidant

When the Heart's a Pasture, and Commitment's Just Another Crop Rotation.

At an agriturismo party on June 11, one I had invited him to, he did not like the pickup time my friend had arranged, and did not have a car at the time.

So instead of telling me, he hitched a ride with some random woman. When he introduced us at the party, I imagine she thought to herself, *What shit did I step into?*

He showed up with her, barely acknowledged me throughout the party, and then told me he had to leave with her, too, because he was hitching a ride to Forte dei Marmi. But, bonus, I should meet him at the beach the next day.

That night, we sat on a garden bench to talk. I was exhausted, mentally, emotionally, spiritually. One single tear slipped out of my eye. One. A tear of sheer frustration, not sadness. I did not want comfort. I wanted clarity.

I keep hoping that if I rattle him hard enough, maybe a single coherent thought will drop down like a prize in a claw machine. Spoiler: I keep losing the claw game.

All he could say was, "Don't cry."
Not, "That was messed up. I see that now."
Just a "Don't cry."

Mop the leak. Never check the pipe.

When he was about to leave, we exchanged a few words in a very public area. After he left, I was approached by a gentleman with whom we exchanged pleasantries. The first thing out of his mouth was that he knew JJ. A lively enough conversation followed, but of course, I was not in the mood to be social; JJ's behavior had already managed to dim the Franciacorta glow of the evening. We exchanged numbers and thought nothing of it.

On the way home, my girlfriend looked over and said compassionately, "I'm sorry he wasn't acting like your boyfriend tonight."

I did not flinch. I said, "That's why he's in therapy."

She blinked. "Is it working?"

I shrugged. "Well… he shows up to the appointment. Emotionally? I think he sends incense."

Over the next few days, it became clear that the man was interested in more than friendship, and I brushed him off. Still, I told JJ that he needed to take ownership in public and stop pretending we did not have a relationship, even if it was complicated.

His response: "Random characters… It's clear that you frequent circles that allow you to make such wonderful acquaintances. Where did you meet them?"

When I told him the man's name, he had no recollection of him at all. My response: "We met at the podere party last Saturday. He knows you because your name came out of his mouth as soon as we started chatting, since he noticed us talking before you left."

By then, I was running low on patience and high on irony. I reminded him that this is the price he pays for going out every night to escape his ghosts. I pointed out that it is the same way he has his therapist's number saved in his phone without remembering how or when it happened, as if she materialized out of smoke.

I was not finished. I told him to stop twisting things around as if I were the one wandering into shady places to meet these "nice characters."

Exhibit 13: Emotional Support Statue, Now Available in Linen Blend

Exhibit Temporarily Closed for Emotional Maintenance.

It was now early July, and my dog had been sick for the last year. She had been in and out of the hospital, pneumonia at first, then constant, expensive maintenance checks, then colitis. That was what finally did her in. At the end, she refused to eat or drink and gave up. We were both exhausted.

Between my trips to Asia and Buenos Aires, I had a three-day layover at home in Florence to switch summer clothes for winter ones and to see JJ, since I had been gone for two weeks. I brought back a lot of things for him from Asia, since he had never been there.

During those three days at home, the dog sitter called me the day before I was supposed to leave for Buenos Aires to say my dog had not eaten in three days. We rushed her to the hospital, and I waited for a diagnosis.

I asked JJ to meet me there. He arrived just in time to see my dog and me in the parking lot. He took us home, and I pushed my Buenos Aires trip out by a week. I ended up spending my birthday in Florence instead of Buenos Aires because my dog was in the hospital.

A couple of days after we were home, my dog was still not eating, and she was no longer standing up. She was lying in places she had never lain before. She had no strength because she was not eating. I called JJ and asked him to come over because I thought it might be time to put her to sleep.

He walked into my flat like a man late to his own performance and immediately started yelling my dog's name, as if volume could summon her back to life. I was sitting quietly on the floor beside her, trying to keep her calm. Her body was weak, she was barely responsive, and I was holding myself together by a thread.

And then came JJ, bellowing her name like he was announcing her onstage at a rock concert. I had to ask him to stop yelling. He said he was trying to get her to stand up. I explained, in disbelief, "You can't yell at a sick creature and expect them to rise to their feet. That's not how love, or biology, works."

He did not have the capacity to read the room. Or the moment.

At the vet's office, the gaps only widened. Ilaria, one of Scarlett's vets, knew Scarlett and me well. She and Francesca had treated my dog throughout the past year, during her many hospital visits. She understood what I was going through and Scarlett's case without me needing to explain anything.

JJ, on the other hand, had known Scarlett for five months, had petted her only two or three times, and without warning decided this was the moment to get combative. He began arguing with Ilaria, too loudly and defensively, about why the dog should be put down, as if he were the one with emotional proximity, clinical training, or any understanding of the situation.

I was embarrassed. Ilaria, who is soft-spoken and intuitive, kept her composure and told him that the person who knows when a dog is ready is the person who lives with her. Me. Not the Jurassic Jackass who showed up mid-crisis and decided to shout the dog back to health.

Then came the worst moment. They took Scarlett to the back to insert the IV port. I was left alone in the room with the weight of what I thought I was about to do. I sat in the only chair in the corner of the exam room, sobbing into my hands. I could not breathe. I could not think. I broke.

JJ was standing across the room, frozen. He stood there for several minutes like a man waiting for instructions on how to behave around grief.

He walked over, but he did not reach for me. He did not bend down to meet me. He did not wrap his arms around me. He just stood next to me.

So, I reached out, wrapped my arms around his waist like a lifeline, and got a statue. A stiff, cold, silent figure who understood conceptually that something should be done but had no idea what it was.

And then, in true JJ fashion, just as Scarlett miraculously walked back into the room, because, spoiler alert, I did not go through with it, he said, "I'm going to the bathroom. I don't feel well."

His system could not handle the weight of genuine grief, real love, or real connection, so he defaulted to his internal panic room: the vet's bathroom.

I did not need a therapist to tell me what was happening. I knew. He was dysregulated, shutting down, and using physical withdrawal to avoid emotional exposure.

And then came another classic JJ reset.

He came back in after several minutes, re-entered the room as if none of it had happened, and began cracking jokes, as if humor were Windex, and he could wipe the scene clean.

But I remember everything.

For the two vet emergency visits, I had given him an ultimatum because he had failed me so many times that I had learned never to rely on him. I drew a line in the sand and told him that if he did not show up, we had nothing more to talk about. And he did.

He did not show up perfectly, but he did show up, and at the time, that counted. The only word he seemed to catch in that sentence was "perfect," accompanied by a deer-in-the-headlights look.

Obviously, he never received that memo, or opened it, skimmed the first line, and filed it under "emotional spam." To this day, he has not grasped the concept, as evidenced by his inability to show up on an agreed day and time for a meeting or, for that matter, an IKEA appointment.

And let's be honest: if you cannot emotionally regulate enough to commit to furniture assembly, the relationship itself does not stand much of a chance.

This is the thing with emotionally stunted people. It is not that they do not care; it is that their internal operating system is so outdated that it crashes under basic emotional tasks.

People like him cannot regulate their emotions, so instead they manage their proximity to other people's emotions: avoid, delay, reschedule, disappear, joke, or freeze. This is not dysfunction that looks like chaos; it is dysfunction disguised as busyness, logistics, or political "emergencies."

Just not on the correct day, at the proper time, in the correct dimension.

Fast forward two months. As soon as I was back from Buenos Aires, my baby was finally home with me, but in very frail condition. I went dark on JJ after he missed my birthday, which was the day before I left on the two-month trip.

The only communication we had after I left was when I cc'd his therapist on *The Letter*, a move that surely rattled the Jurassic nervous system. The subject line was "Last Letter," and the attachment was titled: "JJ and Alessandra." It read like the final exhibit plaque in a museum tour gone off the rails. That was about a week after I left.

What followed was a predictably toxic text from him, defensive, passive-aggressive, and wildly off-key. I left it unanswered. I did not text him again about my keys until mid-September, and I made no mention of Scarlett's passing. I was not going to cloud her memory by dragging him into it.

Nor was I going to invite him to her euthanasia at home. She deserved better than sharing space with his inability to emotionally regulate, or, worse, making it about himself. That time belonged to her. The grief was sacred, and managing his feelings on top of losing my dog would have been like trying to host a funeral while babysitting a velociraptor on a sugar crash.

Exhibit 14: Some Wires Were Never Meant to Connect

Hardware intact. Software is missing.

On July 6, before I left for Argentina, on our way back home from dinner, my blood pressure abruptly dropped while we were walking. I had to sit down on the church steps to catch my breath. He asked if he should call a cab. We were two blocks away; I just needed to sit.

He offered to carry me home, but I said it was not necessary. Any emotionally literate human would have sat beside me and held my hand. But JJ? He was muttering in existential panic, walking around like a lost tour guide in Florence, while I was trying not to faint.

The moment called for quiet presence, but he could not sit with helplessness, his or mine. So instead of joining me on the steps, he conducted a one-man triage drill for a situation that required nothing more than stillness.

Once we got home, he went into full paramedic mode. He made me take my blood pressure ten times and forced water and crackers on me like I had been rescued from a shipwreck. It was not compassion; it was crisis management. It felt somatically similar to what I had experienced at the vet's office.

JJ's version of empathy came with an instruction manual. Unfortunately, it only covered situations involving cables, plugs, or IKEA screws.

Exhibit 15: The Cashless Philosopher

In Which a Simple €1,000 Loan Becomes a Spiritual Lesson on ATM's and Avoidance.

Florence runs on beauty, espresso, and a shocking absence of cash. Western Union here is basically a rumor. I have become so familiar with the cash-pickup staff that I could list them as emergency contacts, except, of course, none of them ever has actual cash.

So, in a rare act of practicality, I asked JJ to lend me €1,000 in cash. Not because I did not have it, I did, but because Florence operates on a barter system between chaos and confusion. I had already sent myself money the night the sitter came to meet Scarlett, only to arrive at the pickup location and be told, "Mi dispiace, no cash today."

Meanwhile, my poor Scarlett had spent most of that week in the hospital while I scrambled to find someone who could take over her care. I was leaving for Buenos Aires in two days, and time was evaporating faster than JJ's promises. The vet, Ilaria, became my unlikely savior, calling in favors as if she were assembling the Avengers of animal care.

The sitter was right there with me, witnessing this tragicomedy unfold. It was his first time meeting me, and by the end of it, he probably thought I was the kind of woman who pays her bills in interpretive dance. He even said, half-jokingly, that Scarlett's situation would make a great case study in abandonment trauma. Poor man, he did not yet know that I would rather sleep at the airport clutching my dog than leave her behind. But his skepticism was understandable; the setting screamed chaos, and JJ's ghostly reliability did not help.

Scarlett's vet found a vet-school dropout who had decided he preferred dog-sitting to dissection. He was available, competent, and willing to take a special-needs dog at the height of summer, a literal unicorn.

So yes, I needed paper money. Fast. Hence, my call to JJ, the one man in Florence guaranteed to turn a simple transaction into a philosophical TED Talk. It was my birthday too, because of course it was. I was not asking him to fund a revolution, just to hand over some paper currency.

Instead, he launched into his usual sermon. Withdrawing money from his business account apparently required divine intervention, a board meeting, and possibly a ceremonial burning of sage. I was not asking for a fiscal audit. I just needed cash. You would think I had requested a kidney.

I suggested he take it from his personal account and that I wire the repayment immediately. A simple plan. Predictably, he evaporated faster than a gelato in July.

And because irony is his native language, he followed up with a story about a time he was in the U.S. and had to pay "expensive fees" to withdraw twenty dollars. An anecdote so detached from my situation it could have been broadcast from the moon.

So, on Saturday morning, before the sitter arrived to collect my baby, I embarked on the Florentine Cash Crawl, a heroic pilgrimage through a series of ATMs, each with its own absurd, minuscule withdrawal limit, hidden service fees, and existential sigh. By the fourth or fifth machine, I felt like a contestant on *Survivor: Banking Edition.*

By noon, I finally had my €1,000, multiple receipts, and a newfound appreciation for medieval barter systems. Scarlett got her sitter. I got my cash. And JJ maintained his unblemished record of spiritual grandstanding over actual usefulness.

Exhibit 16: The Last-Minute Bail: A Two-for-One Disappointment Experience

Missed the birthday. Missed the goodbye. But hey, he toxic-texted... eventually.

The week of my birthday, July 11, I had been in the hospital all week with my baby. JJ showed up twice during that time when I called him to the vet hospital, a personal record in the Museum of Minimal Effort. Given the week I had endured, any decent human would have said, "Your birthday's coming up, and you're leaving tomorrow. Let's do something."

But no.

I had to remind him it was my birthday. He blinked, thought about it, and said, "How are you celebrating?"

How am I celebrating? Like we were two strangers in line at the post office.

I said, "Let's do something," and he replied that he was tired and that, besides, I was supposed to be in Buenos Aires for my birthday.

Martin, a regular in my circle, and another friend were waiting to do a last-minute celebration, but by then, I was not in the mood. Because clearly, birthdays only count if you are geographically convenient. And if avoidance had an Olympic team, he would be the flag bearer.

I was furious, crying, packing, and worried about finding a last-minute dog sitter after spending all week at the hospital. But no. That would have required intimacy and accountability in the same sitting, and his system does not support dual processing.

The very next day, after I left for Buenos Aires, the day after he missed my birthday, JJ decided to double down on emotional absurdity. Bam. Out of nowhere: "Ciao, com'è stai?" accompanied by a couple of random pool photos. Zero context.

I almost spat out my water, caught between disbelief and a laugh dripping with absurdity.

Nothing says *I'm totally fine ignoring your birthday* like sending thirst-trap selfies from the shallow end of avoidance. The pool, as always, was shallow, a fitting metaphor.

This was real-time damage control. He did not reach out because he cared; he reached out because he felt the shift, the emotional current pulling away from him. He knew he had detonated something significant, something structural, and his instinct was to rush in, not to rebuild, but to repaint the rubble.

This time, though, his attempt at a quick reset only made the silence louder.

Exhibit 17: You Had One Job, The Pet Edition

Starring JJ, the man who couldn't fetch dog medication but could fetch emotional chaos.

Before I left for Asia in June, I made what I thought was a simple, responsible decision: I gave him a copy of my keys. I had no idea this would become a flagship exhibit and a cornerstone artifact in the Museum of Dysfunction, inspiring its own line of commemorative gift-shop merch.

Because my baby had been in poor health for the past year, I wanted someone local in case of an emergency. Two months in Buenos Aires, right after a trip to Asia, and practicality demanded an emergency contact. What could possibly go wrong?

Everything went fine for the first sit. Then came the long haul, also known as Colitis & the City. My sweet Burrito, the self-stuffing sausage of joy who would eat until she exploded, suddenly stopped eating altogether. That was my first clue that something was wrong, because this was a dog who considered floor crumbs a five-course meal.

The sitter left her lying in her own urine, which earned Scarlett not only burns on her rear leg but a permanent spot in my nightmares. Add arthritis, a new renal diet because of ailing kidneys, and a heavy medication schedule, and you have the canine equivalent of a geriatric ICU.

The first sitter, Susanna, must have been administering pills like a blackjack dealer, fast, forceful, and missing the emotional context, until my poor girl shut down her appetite in protest.

By the time I flew back through Florence, I learned that Scarlett had not eaten for three days. Cue the emergency vet hospital and my full transformation into a rescue mission in heels.

Fast-forward to July 20: the day the keyholder made his grand cameo. I asked if he was in Florence because the new sitter needed extra medication, specifically Cerenia, which, at roughly twenty dollars a tablet, is essentially canine caviar. I knew I had a few tablets left at home. I needed him to hand them over.

He replied that he was "out of Florence." Fine. I asked when he would be back. He said, "Maybe the 23rd, but I'm not one hundred percent sure." So, I clarified, "When will you know?" Then I spoon-fed him a response template like I was training a toddler: If not by Wednesday, then by Friday. I'll keep you updated.

In classic Jurassic Jackass fashion, he delivered his signature fog-machine reply: "I will most certainly be back in about ten days, or maybe more. In the meantime, if Scarlett needs any medication, I suggest you send the list to the dog sitter."

I thanked him, sarcastically, of course, with a "Thank you for your help," which ricocheted off his prehistoric skull without leaving so much as a dent.

Thus concluded the moment, a neat summary proving that JJ could not retrieve twenty-dollar pills to save a dog's stomach, but could retrieve endless excuses, self-importance, and a starring role in the Museum's Hall of Unmet Expectations.

Exhibit 18: The Great Therapy Escape – Where Accountability Checks In, and JJ Checks Out.

When Accountability Books a Spa Day.

By the start of my Buenos Aires trip, JJ had been in therapy for about eight weeks, and I decided it was time for the actual exhibit.

So, I sent him *The Letter*.

And because this museum values educational outreach, I sent the same one to his therapist. Consider it a joint-sponsored intervention between the Department of Emotional Accountability and the Institute for Chronically Avoidant Adults.

The exhibit itself was titled: **"Take this pattern to therapy, because from the outside, you look emotionally unstable."**

It was part relationship autopsy, part masterclass in pattern recognition, and part public service announcement.

Some women send postcards from their trips. I sent diagnostic exhibits.

The Texts After the Pool Photos

Curator's Text, July 15

Bring this pattern to therapy, because from the outside, you seem unstable, and it's exhausting.

On July 12, the day after my birthday, you sent me a series of pool photos with no context whatsoever. Then you texted, "How are you?" as if nothing had happened.

This was the day after our emotional clash on my birthday, and the night before my departure.

No acknowledgment. No repair. Just "serene" images, as if nothing had taken place.

That isn't emotional balance; it's dissociation. It's an attempt to mask a rupture with aesthetics and silence.

And this is exactly the pattern that makes you seem unstable, because stable people don't send postcards while the fire is still burning.

Unstable people, especially avoidant ones like you, build relationships that move in circles, not forward. When I try to move ahead, you freeze. When I try to go deeper, you withdraw. When I ask for coherence, you offer crumbs disguised as gestures.

You've lived in a relationship built on resets, not resolutions, and that ends now.

You feel everything, but when it matters, you vanish, like on my birthday, and like the night before my long trip. You avoid conflict, get lost in details, or pretend nothing happened. That's not affection; it's emotional cowardice.

Your empathy means nothing if you keep using it to avoid responsibility. If you can't face discomfort, then all that "feeling" becomes another way to control the outcome. I don't need sweetness; I need strength. The kind of strength that shows up when it's hard, not just when it's comfortable.

Until you learn to stay, especially when you want to run, nothing you feel will have value. Not for me. Not for us. That's the version of you that real love requires.

I'm not here to repeat this pattern forever. I'm here to name it, call it what it is, and leave you with the responsibility to do something about it, not pretend that small gestures fix everything.

Avoiding honest conversations doesn't erase pain; it adds dishonesty and emotional whiplash. I'm not punishing you. But I've stopped tolerating these passive, indirect patterns. If you want to grow, this must be the focus of your therapy.

You need accountability, reliability, coherence, and repair. Otherwise, you'll keep losing the people who care about you. I've faced this pattern more times than is healthy for me, but I'll leave before it turns me bitter, dull, or numb. If you want access to me, you'll have to show up as a stable, reliable human being.

This version of you? I won't carry it anymore. Please bring it to therapy tomorrow.

JJ's Text, July 16

Tomorrow I won't go to her, but on the 23rd. I hope we'll remain friends! You know I care about you very much, but I don't want to have a romantic relationship. Love goes far beyond the physical relationship. It's a broad and profound concept that often comes closer to friendship than to romantic relationships. I hug you tight and wish you a good vacation. In the meantime, I'll continue my journey. Kisses.

The Letter, July 22

Sometimes you make me laugh, your ridiculousness, your absurdity, and your complete detachment from reality.

You think your polite tone and pseudo-reflections make you sound emotionally intelligent. This isn't enlightenment; it's the moment you're being asked to take responsibility.

The truth is, you're fundamentally detached from emotional reality. You're like a boy trying to navigate a fire with a scented candle.

You quote Rumi-style phrases like "Love goes far beyond the physical relationship," forgetting that you couldn't even show up for my birthday, which, by the way, was the night before my eight-week trip. Sir, please take a seat. Your "broad and profound concept" of love didn't survive a dinner invitation.

You're a walking disaster, scattering breadcrumbs and dodging philosophy.

It's like a TED Talk and an emotional ghost had a baby. LOL.

But I don't think we can be friends. There's no possibility, and here's why:

Even without the damage you caused, a friendship with you would be useless in its emotional hunger.

What would it be? Superficial updates? Polite messages pretending our story meant nothing? A dynamic where I keep giving more, only now under the label of "friend"? Or just another name you've collected in your phone among the thousands you barely remember?

There would still be no depth. No nourishment. Just breadcrumbs in a new package. You know I hate wasting my time on shallow relationships, even friendships. If I already felt lonely next to you, why would I want to feel lonely in a friendship with you?

For heaven's sake, you couldn't show up for me, or deliver my dog's medication to the sitter, or show up to therapy the moment I left.

And unfortunately, that's exactly why you'll never achieve your supposed goal of having a family or keeping a girlfriend, because you have no emotional courage.

Life expands or contracts in proportion to one's courage. That's why your life is so small.

It's full of superficial relationships and "friendships" with people you marginally remember, names in your contact list. You go out five or six nights a week, convincing yourself you're "living your best life," but really, you're running.

This pattern isn't about pleasure; it's about distraction, dissociation, and avoiding the emotional weight you refuse to process. When you feel overwhelmed by attachment stress, shame, or perceived failure, you don't move closer to intimacy or reflection. You flee.

Avoidant people like you aren't emotionless; they're overwhelmed by emotions but haven't developed the skills to live with that discomfort. So, superficial social stimulation becomes your drug of choice.

You live a damned double life. That curated social life is a costume you wear to convince yourself you're not falling apart. But the more validation you chase, the emptier you feel, and the lonelier the vicious circle becomes.

So instead of facing the consequences of the relational damage you've caused, the birthday disaster, not picking me up at the train station, you avoid the responsibility and shame that come from admitting, "I hurt someone I care about, and I don't know how to make it right."

You had the chance to break that vicious circle with me and build something with the depth and intimacy you claim to want so desperately.

I didn't flinch when I met the demons you've spent your whole life running from. I chose to stay and fight them with you. But you chose emotional cowardice at the one time in your life when someone real showed up.

I'm so tired of being your de facto therapist and writing this bullshit since February. I don't know what else to do to wake you up, for fuck's sake.

All I know is that when all this is over, and you leave me among the rubble, picking up the pieces and cleaning up your mess again, there will be no more contact between us, not even as friends.

If you want to salvage anything and speed up the expensive therapy you're paying for, this letter will get you there faster. I've sent a copy of this letter to Alessandra.

Good luck.

And then, I put my phone down.

Because there's nothing left to say when the conversation has already drowned in the kiddie pool of avoidance.

Analysis: The "Friendship as Spiritual Detour" Defense

His text reads like a dissertation titled *How to End a Relationship Without Ever Saying the Word Breakup.*

"Tomorrow I won't go to her, but on the 23rd."
He opens by rescheduling accountability, a preemptive strike of procrastination disguised as logistics. Therapy delayed is therapy denied.

"I hope we can remain friends."
Avoidant code for "I don't want to feel guilty." Friendship becomes emotional insurance, a way to downgrade intimacy without canceling access.

"I care about you, but I don't want a romantic relationship."
Translation: I want the benefits of your emotional labor without the responsibility of reciprocity.

> "Love goes far beyond the physical relationship."

Ah, yes, Plato with Wi-Fi. When avoidants feel cornered, they hide behind abstract nouns.

> "It's a broad and profound concept…"

Translation: If I define love vaguely enough, I can back away while maintaining moral high ground.

> "I send you a big hug…"

Because nothing says closure like a digital hug from the man who couldn't show up in person.

> "I will continue my journey."

The avoidant's favorite euphemism for wandering in emotional circles while congratulating himself for growth.

Curator's Note: A masterclass in detachment, the written equivalent of walking backward out of a room while quoting Rumi.

Shortly after this exchange, his therapist told me she understood my position, that JJ was on his own journey, and that they would address the issues I raised when he was ready.

So, after two months of therapy, he was using the couch like a spa day: horizontal, relaxed, basking in the aromatherapy of his own excuses—no accountability in sight.

I received a toxic text shortly thereafter, which I forwarded immediately to his therapist. All communication ceased until I returned and began asking for my keys in mid-September.

Toxic Text Exchange, July 29, 2025

JJ:
Ciao Francesca, com'è stai? I read your letter and agree with some things and disagree with others. But it is not my intention to say what I agree or disagree with, because they are just points of view and opinions. Another person would have considered your intervention highly invasive of privacy, and indeed it was, but I try to grasp the positive, constructive intent of your gesture, made in good faith, even if with excessive ease and in the wrong way. I understand your desire to do good in your own way. I hope you are well and happy in Argentina. Warm regards.

Me:
Silence.

Bonus Material: Lost in Avoidance, The Translator's Cut

JJ: "Ciao Francesca, come stai?"

Translation: I'm opening with a calm, neutral greeting to look composed. Not because I care how you are, but because it sets the tone that I'm the reasonable one here.

JJ: "I read your letter, and I agree with some things and disagree with others."

Translation: I'm refusing to take accountability. By blurring everything into vague "points of view," I neutralize your concrete facts into mere "opinions," making us appear equally responsible.

JJ: "But it is not my intention to say what I agree or disagree with because they are points of view and opinions."

Translation: I'm dodging specifics so I don't have to engage with anything uncomfortable. I'm performing detachment to maintain control, avoiding the conversation while pretending it's philosophical.

JJ: "Know another person would've considered your intervention very invasive of privacy, and indeed it was…"

Translation: Here comes the passive-aggressive sting. I'm moralizing about your "invasion" to punish you for holding me accountable. This is a mild shaming tactic disguised as objectivity.

JJ: "…but I try to grasp the positive and constructive intent of your gesture, made in good faith, even if excessive ease and in the wrong way."

Translation: I'm pretending to be gracious while quietly calling you clumsy, overreaching, and misguided. This is an ego balm. I get to feel generous while still positioning you as the problem.

JJ: "I understand your desire to do good in your own way."

Translation: I'm reducing your intentional, courageous act to a naïve "desire to do good." It's condescending, like patting a child on the head for trying.

JJ: "I hope you are well and happy in Argentina. Warm regards."

Translation: I'm closing the door while implying the matter is resolved. This is how I silence you without engaging your truth. The tone reads like a PR statement: emotionally empty, ethically sanitized, and entirely self-protective.

Little did I know he'd dropped out of therapy shortly after sending this toxic text.

The irony? His therapist already had the receipts.

I found out, in passing, when I got back while trying to retrieve my keys. She blinked, sighed, and said something that could only be translated as: *Ah, yes. My missing patient slash, your missing keys. How poetic.*

At this point, the keys had a better chance of finishing therapy than he did.

Exhibit 19: The Bounty Hunter and the Fossil

The Art of Almost Going.

On September 30, I sent his therapist another text:

It's been two weeks, and I still haven't gotten my keys back. He responds to other messages, but not to my calls or anything related to my keys. This logistical task demonstrates his pathological paralysis when it comes to taking responsibility for anything involving me.

The keys are just the latest example in a long series of failures that demonstrate his paralysis toward me, especially when it comes to intimacy and responsibility.

On Monday, I asked him for my keys for the fourth time and teased him. He said, "Yes, we will see each other," and when I asked *when*, he went silent without delay. When there's responsibility involved, such as setting a time, he freezes.

His avoidance and freezing have never been this severe, so I hope this means he's close to a breakthrough.

It's essential for me that JJ goes to therapy every week. He cannot go biweekly because he is so frozen, and the dysfunction spills over into my life. Please maintain a weekly structure with him.

Simply put: no weekly therapy equals no relationship. If he goes casually, I'm out. He can't do something as simple as giving me back my keys.

Therapist's response:

I don't know why all your messages arrived all at once, including those dated September 14 and 21; that's why I didn't reply. JJ is not coming to therapy. We said goodbye in July with the intention of meeting again in September, but so far, he hasn't contacted me to schedule another appointment. So, I don't know how to help you.

JJ treats therapy like it's a bounty hunter. He doesn't miss appointments; he evades them.

You'd think Alessandra, his therapist, was armed with a tranquilizer gun and a clipboard. Every session becomes a covert operation: *He was last seen near self-awareness at 14:00 but fled on foot when accountability approached.*

He schedules therapy the way other people schedule dental cleanings, far enough in advance to sound committed, but always with an exit strategy. "Next week" is his emotional safe word. He'll say things like, "I'll go on the 23rd," as if naming a future date automatically counts as progress.

For JJ, therapy isn't a process; it's a concept. An abstract painting titled *Intention Without Execution*. He believes merely discussing therapy is emotionally equivalent to attending it. It's as if saying "I have therapy soon" releases enough psychic energy to justify another month of avoidance.

If there were a Fitbit for self-work, Jurassic Jackass would read forty-three steps and a nap.

In the Museum of Dysfunction, his portrait hangs under a spotlight, accompanied by a plaque.

Exhibit 20: The Courtroom of Convenience – Where Half a Day Is Too High a Price for Empathy?

A Case Study in Emotional Labor vs. Actual Labor.

11 September.

My last apartment came with a landlord who immediately decided to major in creative accounting. When I moved out, he kept €1,200 of my security deposit to back-charge me for condo fees in arrears, seven months after I had already moved out.

He'd apparently discovered math and thought he'd try it out on me, with his secretary attempting to bully me under the authority of his title of *Conte*, which made me laugh at the irony that they couldn't count.

I explained, slowly, politely, that they couldn't do that, because they had accepted my rent every single month for a year with the condo fees already rolled in. No objections. No notes. No "by the way, you owe us an extra hundred euros." Nothing. Then, one day: surprise. Retroactive capitalism.

I've worked as a real estate broker and appraiser for over twenty years in Manhattan, and this was ludicrous. This would never stand up in housing court.

It was especially hilarious that *Il Conte*, yes, the landlord with an actual noble title, was offended when I suggested that charging me condo fees in arrears, seven months after I vacated the property, was opportunistic.

Clearly, calling out financial piracy is rude when committed by someone whose ancestors probably taxed peasants for existing.

He clutched his metaphorical pearls, aghast that a mere tenant would accuse nobility of something so… pedestrian. I half expected him to duel me with a fountain pen or summon a herald to announce:

"The Lady of the Lease hath insulted His Deposital Highness!"

Meanwhile, I stood there with receipts, bank transfers, and common sense, none of which are recognized currencies in the Royal House of Florentine Accounting.

So, I told JJ.

This was the first contact I'd had with him since leaving for Buenos Aires in July. As a landlord himself, he agreed with me and said not to pay it. For a brief, dangerous moment, I thought, *Finally—someone on my team.*

Then he asked if I needed an attorney.

I said yes and made a gentle entry to let him know I would also need my spare keys back.

And just like that, the idea evaporated into the Florentine air, joining the other lost causes and unreturned keys.

When I later asked if he would come with me to court and help translate, I received a thirty-minute TED Talk on logistics, time management, and the delicate balance of his schedule, all culminating in a definitive "no," because it would waste half a day.

This was also the day he asked me if Scarlett had passed away.

I never mentioned it to him. Nor did I call him for any kind of support.

Flash forward one month.

I met a wonderful young man and asked if he could drive and translate for me. Without missing a beat, he said, "I can take you to the courthouse and IKEA on Thursday. Does that work?"

That's the difference right there.

One man gives you a thesis on inconvenience.

The other gives you a time slot and a ride.

One promises therapy and delivers excuses.

The other shows up, chauffeurs, translates, and buys me a sandwich.

Exhibit 21: The IKEA Emotional Assembly Kit - Arrives flat-packed, with Missing Emotional Components. Screws not included.

Some assembly required; accountability sold separately.

I asked JJ if he could drive me to IKEA so I could get pricing on three closet models I was interested in.

Of course, planning anything with him more than three days out is the classic Italian version of vediamo logistics.

With JJ, it's amplified by internal chaos. Even without dysfunction, Italians generally operate on a short planning horizon. Add his avoidance tendencies, and you get a man who combusts if you ask for a date more than seventy-two hours in advance.

At this stage, it wasn't about me at all. It was about the total short-circuit inside him. The part that should generate a simple yes, no, or thank-you response was jammed by fear, shame, and avoidance. His silence wasn't punishment or strategy; it was collapse.

So, my instinct was to keep things practical but open-ended. Let me know what day and time. I gave him structure that still felt breathable. Not pressure, just options.

My text gave him several possible days. Since I didn't know how long it would take to price out three models and pick up a few items from the warehouse floor, I suggested an appointment toward the end of the day. That way, he wouldn't be late for subsequent appointments, and it wouldn't be a wasted trip rushed by anxiety.

Again, he went silent for a day or two.

I sent him a text that said, "Please seek help. You are not a bad person, but you are a man so trapped in your avoidance that basic respect becomes impossible."

Him: "It doesn't mean I need help because I don't reply straight away. I was out at a concert."

Me:
"You manage the optics. Instead of saying something simple and human, like "Sorry, I'm out, can we talk tomorrow?" you rush to prove that you're not the problem. That reflex, to defend yourself rather than connect, is pure shame avoidance.

That's the problem.

You try to manage perception instead of the relationship. Your goal is to prove you are not a bad person rather than to prove you can be a reliable one. Your reflex is not to connect, repair, or reassure, but to protect, explain, and justify. Every time your shame kicks in, your empathy switches off."

If he managed to answer closer to the day with something precisely on brand for him, that was fine. The goal wasn't German-level scheduling. It was follow-through at all.

At this point, the museum exhibit was half built.

If he booked the IKEA slot or confirmed midweek, that would be a small miracle of executive functioning by his standards. Nothing says adulthood like needing a confirmed appointment to beg for furniture you'll assemble yourself and probably swear at.

He managed to confirm the day before, after I asked when he could take me. He then asked why I didn't remember.

The problem was that he never confirmed which day to begin with.

It had originally been for the past Tuesday, but I told him I was just coming back from France, so it would have to be toward the end of the week. That was the part that was never confirmed.

Classic Jurassic Jackass move: gaslight-adjacent memory rewrite.

He implied I forgot something that was never confirmed, shifting the burden, quietly, onto me instead of his inconsistency.

This is part of his phantom planning pattern: he makes vague half-mentions, then employs retroactive framing, as we already said, to mask avoidant indecision.

I had to lie down for a nap after trying to organize something as simple as an IKEA trip, which always turns into an Olympic event of calendar confusion, emotional gymnastics, and multiple rounds of "Wasn't this already confirmed?"

Then, yet again, the night before, after we had agreed on a time and I had sent over a screenshot of our IKEA appointment, which he had acknowledged eight hours earlier, I received a panicked voice note at 8:30 p.m.

He said I had chosen a time that didn't suit him, and that if I wanted, he could accompany me at a time that suited him instead. A time he claimed he had already told me about.

My response: I asked you what time. You didn't respond. So, I booked a time.

He had told me the day before that we could go tomorrow. But he never confirmed an actual day when I said, "Sometime, toward the end of the week, we can go."

And it was the only time IKEA had available, because he waited until the last minute, as usual.

The man couldn't even lock down an IKEA reschedule. Confirmation that he was still operating on **Jurassic Jackass Standard Time™**, where accountability is extinct, and scheduling is a lost art.

I calmly texted him to ask which day he could take me and told him I would reschedule the appointment accordingly.

It was like emotional Sudoku, except the numbers kept changing and the instructions were written in hieroglyphics.

His response:
"I didn't wait until the last minute. I told you right away that I could do it during my lunch break. I have a working life too; it's not like I'm on permanent holiday. I'll let you know at the end of the day. But I was only available during the week at the time I told you and made it clear."

Me:
"That's why the end of the working day is better for both of us. It's less disruptive to our schedules. They close at 8 p.m., or the weekend is fine."

Jurassic Jackass Translations

JJ: "I didn't wait until the last minute."
Meaning: Defensive denial to avoid guilt.
Translation: *Yes, I did, but I don't like how it feels when you point it out calmly, and I can't argue.*

JJ: "I told you right away I could do it during lunch."
Translation: *The least convenient possible time for you.*
Thirty minutes there and back. Ten minutes from parking to wardrobes. Unknown appointment length. Rushed. Stressed. Why? Because chaos is his love language.

JJ: "I have a working life too; it's not like I'm on permanent holiday."
Motive: Passive dig.

Translation: *I feel inferior and don't know how to manage it, so I'll try to knock you down instead of communicating.*

JJ: "I'll let you know at the end of the day."
Translation: Delay tactic. Still no commitment. Never committed. Classic Jurassic Jackass frozen in the permafrost, hoping the problem evaporates.

JJ: "I was only available at the time I told you and made clear."
Purpose: Emotional absolution attempt.
Reality: I asked for clarity multiple times. He never confirmed. His ego doesn't like being held to a timeline.

Crickets.

Follow-Up Text

"Dear JJ,

You suggest lunch because it's a short meeting with a built-in escape route. Emotionally safe. If things stay light, you can continue your day. But if they get serious, *Oh, lunch break is over, I have to run.*

This is emotional triage disguised as scheduling.

Only being available for an hour isn't time management, it's emotional perimeter control. You're terrified that if you stay, you might feel something too deep, or worse, have to answer for your behavior.

If you can drop me with thirty minutes' notice, you can cancel or postpone your superficial Florentine fan club. Let's not pretend this is about time.

You're afraid of the unknown when you're with me, because unlike those safe, superficial social engagements, I see you."

And that mirror terrifies the Jurassic Jackass.

This is why he freezes and keeps proposing one-hour meetings. I'm the unfinished business he can't ghost.

JJ's concept of time management exists in the same dimension as Minotaurs and mutual accountability, rumored, periodically discussed, but never actually sighted. To him, a schedule is an oppressive colonial construct designed to restrict his *flow*.

He either confirms a proper time and walks into the meeting with his tail between his metaphorical legs, proposes another escape hatch and exposes the loop to himself, or ghost-dances straight into irrelevance.

We can consider this exhibit closed.

Exhibit 22: Flat-Packed, Missing Screws, The Universe Has a Sense of Humor

Because apparently even furniture avoids commitment.

I thought the IKEA metaphor had already reached peak irony when I named the exhibit: The IKEA Emotional Assembly Kit: Arrives flat-packed, with missing emotional parts. Screws not included. But apparently, the universe heard me and said, "Challenge accepted."

Because when the actual IKEA bookshelf arrived, there it was: pristine panels, crisp instructions, zero hardware. Not a single screw. Just a lonely bag of air where accountability should've been.

I stood there laughing like a woman who's seen too much. After all, how poetic is it that the physical manifestation of Jurassic Jackass logistics showed up at my doorstep, literally incapable of being assembled?

It was as if the Italians at the factory collectively decided, "Vediamo… maybe she doesn't need the screws." Which, to be fair, is the same planning philosophy JJ has lived by since 1982.

Austria never did this to me. The USA never did this to me. Only in Italy can you receive an entire bookshelf with the emotional equivalent of, "Good luck, Cara, build character instead."

At that point, I didn't even want the screws. I wanted a museum plaque: "Some Exhibits Build Themselves. Others Fall Apart Gracefully."

Because, honestly, how do you top the cosmic comedy of life imitating a metaphor that imitates IKEA?

Exhibit 23: The Pompeii of Keys: Frozen in Avoidance

A domestic artifact left behind in the ruins of what should've been simple.

Sometime around mid-September, I mentioned that I would need my spare keys back soon. He went glazed entirely, like someone hit "force quit" on his empathy app.

By 20 September, I tried again: "Umm... my keys?" No response.

Five days later, I texted to see if he was out. He said, "I was out earlier." A non-answer worthy of a hostage negotiation transcript.

By 30 September, I'd lost patience and asked if he was still seeing his therapist, Alessandra. He replied: "Right now I'm seeing priests."

Of course, he is. Because why seek professional help when you can go full Vatican on your emotional problems? I snapped back at him, "You don't need priests, you need fucking therapy."

He dodged my calls and texts about my keys or therapy.

Then came the pièce de résistance, the spiritual text: "Francesca, I am convinced that what must happen will happen and that I must undertake a spiritual journey of self-discovery."

I barked, "You need therapy, not fucking discovery!"

By 4 October, he texted, "Ok, I need therapy and will do it." A bold promise, and, like the keys, entirely theoretical.

By 10 October, I asked again. He sent me photos of about fifty random keys, saying he didn't know which were mine because he had "a million keys," including those of his relatives. He's a landlord, and he doesn't know which keys belong to whom? I detect a stall tactic.

The man could single-handedly star in CSI: Locksmith Confusion. It's now 26 October, and still, no keys…and counting. It has been going on for 6 weeks of filming this absurdity.

I studied his photo collage as if it were a Rorschach test for dysfunction. Some keys I knew instantly that they weren't mine, but one looked somewhat familiar. I sent it to him, saying I thought it might be mine, but I'd have to test it to be sure.

Because getting my own keys back now requires a laboratory trial, a spiritual awakening, and a fucking miracle.

JJ's refusal to return my keys was never just about the metal itself. It was about control, avoidance, and the unbearable discomfort of closure. To most people, keys are practical objects that grant access. To him, they carry emotional weight, symbolizing intimacy and trust. Giving them back would have required a final act of accountability and closure, a small but undeniable acknowledgment that something had ended.

For someone like JJ, that kind of finality is intolerable. It disrupts the illusion of indefinite options, of keeping emotional doors propped open "just in case." Returning my keys would have meant admitting that the relationship, in its former form, no longer existed. And that acknowledgment would require a level of maturity and self-confrontation he wasn't capable of.

His silence, his vague replies, and his photo of dozens of indistinguishable keys all spoke to the same pattern. He wasn't confused about which keys were mine. He was avoiding what they represented: the end of entitlement, the loss of control, and the quiet reckoning that comes when there's nothing left to delay.

In the end, the keys became a perfect metaphor for him: a simple act turned impossible, a gesture that would have closed a chapter but instead became its own exhibit in the museum of unfinished business.

Even his care package, which has sat in my flat, weighed less than accountability, was in a paper bag with approximately 1 kilogram of missed opportunities, and was easily delivered by our common housekeeper.

In yet another dazzling display of overcomplication, I sent him a soft, illustrated example of how easy this could be: a neatly neutral, logistics-approved third party like our housekeeper who could deliver his care package/food bag (which, by the way, had been living rent-free in my apartment since July).

All he had to do was give him my keys since he was at my place a couple of times a week, cleaning and assembling furniture. That's it. A transaction so light it didn't even weigh ten pounds. I wasn't asking him to move a sofa, just his conscience.

At this point, I poke his dysfunction for sport like a hemorrhoid because it is an inflamed spot he refuses to treat.

He can pretend he's fine, but the moment I touch the sore point (keys, accountability, closure), he winces and goes silent. It's a perfect metaphor: chronic, irritating, entirely self-inflicted, and made worse by sitting in his denial too long.

Yet, somehow, this modest errand turned into an existential challenge. If emotional maturity were measured in kilos, this would've been a three-gram request, and he still couldn't lift it.

It's as if handing over keys through the cleaner would have triggered a full-body allergic reaction to closure. So instead, the keys stayed, and my patience took an unscheduled sabbatical.

Exhibit 24: Panic at 3 p.m. – The Collapse of Scheduled Intimacy

When emotional proximity triggers a fire drill.

We were supposed to meet at my place since I hadn't seen him in almost four months.

I gave him two full days' notice for a simple 7:00 p.m. conversation, not a proposal, not a crisis summit, just two adults speaking in a private, safe space. He agreed. No hesitation. At 10 a.m. on the day itself, he checked in with composure: "Are we still seeing each other tonight?" I was delightfully surprised and replied, "Yes." For a moment, I let myself believe we were finally entering the realm of adult follow-through.

Then came 3:00 p.m.

Right on cue, the panic arrived. I received not one but two virtually identical voice notes, each a panicked scramble of rescheduling suggestions. Coffee? Lunch? Something "more convenient"? His tone was frayed, flooded. His nervous system had entered full red alert, and the meeting, once a simple, agreed-upon plan, now loomed as a perceived emotional ambush. I knew it was happening. I'd seen this movie before.

By 6:30 p.m., he pulled the emergency eject cord: a sudden change of venue. Instead of meeting at my place, since he said he would suggest a place, but didn't propose a place, he proposed we meet at a random bar near Santa Maria Novella for one hour, 30 minutes before the scheduled time because of an alleged last-minute political commitment that had somehow just materialized, a commitment he obviously would've known about two days earlier when we made the plan.

This wasn't a logistical adjustment. It was the behavioral choreography of someone trying to dodge intimacy while maintaining the illusion of engagement. He was laying the groundwork for me to cancel, so he could tell himself he had tried. That's the real trick here.

If I cancel, he keeps a clean conscience. He gets to say, "Well, I offered to meet," while avoiding the deeper reality: he couldn't handle the emotional proximity of being alone with me in my space, on my terms, without distraction, mask, or escape route.

He asked me if I was coming, and I flat-out said, "No." I'm not getting dressed, walking all the way over there for him to meet me for an hour. Told him not to squeeze me in, and I am not a roadshow like his political party events.

And this time, I didn't bend. I didn't run to meet him at the bar or salvage a plan he'd already gutted. I didn't fall for the one-hour consolation prize. No, is a complete sentence.

When I retold the story to my friends in France, over wine, with zero context, they saw right through the charade. "Ah," one said, mid-sip. "So, he didn't cancel. He delegated the cancellation." Delegated like a man who's afraid of confrontation but intensely committed to self-preservation.

The idea of sitting across from me in a room built for honesty triggers something in him he can't explain. And rather than sit with the discomfort, he manufactures chaos, last-minute venue swaps, vague emergencies, until he can convince himself he's off the hook. It's not avoidance. It's a performance of effort designed to dodge actual presence.

I almost forgot how vehemently allergic the Jurassic Jackass is to actual intimacy, until I remembered that, in all the time we were dating and allegedly "connected," he never once came to my house alone for dinner. Not once. Not even when I dangled it like a low-stakes invitation wrapped in pasta and dim lighting, I got silence.

Being a retired Culinary Institute of America chef turned museum curator means I can braise your trauma and label it Exhibit A. And in all my years, I've never had a single boyfriend who didn't want to eat at my place... until this one.

The man managed to resist a Michelin-level meal as if it were an emotional boundary. Who turns down dinner from a CIA-trained chef? Obviously, someone who's also fasting from accountability and intimacy.

I guess he's allergic to coming to dinner at my house alone. The poor man breaks out in hives at the thought of emotional proximity served warm. It was as if walking through my front door unaccompanied would trigger some ancient curse that turned him to stone, which, to be fair, he was already halfway to most of the time.

I could've cooked him a Michelin-star meal, and he'd still claim a mysterious "energy imbalance" or that his inner child wasn't ready to digest homemade affection. For him, dining one-on-one is less of a "romantic evening" and more of "exposure therapy." If intimacy were gluten, JJ would need an EpiPen.

Now compare that to the young man I occasionally see, a functional adult male with working emotional Wi-Fi. The moment I say I'm cooking dinner and might invite a few friends, he doesn't flinch or stall. He smiles and says, "Actually, I'd rather it be just the two of us."

And when I go to turn off the light at night? He stops me and says, "Wait a minute... I want to look at your beautiful face."

Night and day. Velociraptor versus an actual human man. One avoids eye contact as if it owed him money; the other treats connection like dessert.

And to think I once thought JJ was "deep" when in fact, he was emotionally constipated with poetic flair.

Psychologically, this is textbook emotional sabotage. It's the classic disorganized-avoidant double feature: terrified of closeness, petrified of loss, and somehow managing to chase both at once like a malfunctioning Roomba of intimacy.

This isn't repair; it's "I tried" becomes a press release, every "you walked away" a rebrand. It's dysfunction with a customer service smile, the kind of sabotage that arrives gift-wrapped, stamped "Good Intentions Inside."

In short, he's not fixing the problem. He's redecorating the crime scene.

Exhibit 25: The Invisible Vacation: How to Be Away Without Leaving Home

Now Boarding: Flight Avoidance 101, Nonstop to Nowhere.

This is what he said, after I told him yet again when a good day and time would be to pick up my keys.

Him: "Ciao Francesca, if you want, we can meet for a coffee after lunch on Wednesday or Thursday at a bar. I'll bring you what keys I have. I'm not sure they're the right ones, but you can check when you get home."

Translation: "I would like to stage-manage accountability in a public setting with caffeine and plausible deniability."

The "bar" setting is peak JJ, a neutral zone with just enough espresso to simulate civility, yet far enough from my flat to prevent the sudden outbreak of closure. He's back in town, of course, but the man treats his location like state secrets: half spy, one hundred percent Jurassic Jackass, pulling his signature move, hiding behind imaginary curtains, yelling, "You can't see me!" while his big feet and tail are sticking out like a sore thumb.

While this was happening, I was ready to handle this like an adult, post-chiropractor, relaxed spine, calm energy, ring the bell, retrieve the keys, and leave. No drama, no espresso diplomacy. Because if he's home, he can't play "I'm away." And if he's not… well, at least I've filed another official attempt in the ongoing documentary titled "The Case of the Missing Keys: A Study in Avoidant Cartography."

The Jurassic Jackass Time-Space Continuum strikes again, where he can be concurrently "out of town," "on his way back," and "available for coffee in centro," depending on which version of reality keeps him safest from accountability.

He's like Schrödinger's Boyfriend: both home and away until you ring the bell and collapse the quantum wave of avoidance.

The "I'm away" routine is just emotional bubble wrap, so he doesn't have to face me until he can stage-manage the encounter (public place, coffee, plausible deniability).

It's the same move as: "I can't possibly hand over your keys today… because I'm in an undisclosed region of Avoidanceland."

Then, like clockwork, he reappears with, "If you want, we can meet for a coffee…" as if he just materialized from a spirit quest instead of dodging a doorbell.

Ladies and gentlemen, welcome to the Flight Gate of Eternal Excuses. Our featured traveler, JJ, is once again "out of town this weekend," venturing where accountability dares not go. Rumor has it he's joined Buck Rogers on an intergalactic layover somewhere between "Vediamo Prime" and "Planet Postpone." His mission: to explore new worlds, avoid emotional confrontation, and never, under any circumstances, return the keys.

In the Departure Hall of Dysfunction, you'll find a display of his vintage itineraries.

My Italian guy friend, who works in tech and teaches at Stanford University, said, "What, no keys after 6 weeks and he's a landlord?!" Even a calm, rational, tech-genius crowd sees how absurd this is. Six weeks of key returns would confuse an entire engineering department!

Exhibit 26: Florentine Doorbell Diplomacy: When Closure Becomes a Crime

Part-Time Landlord, Full-Time Escape Artist.

Pivoting to another topic, I did something I would generally never do. I called him at 12:30 a.m. to see if he was home. As I was walking home from a party at 1:30 a.m., I rang his bell, merely because I was nearby. Naturally, I thought he was not home. But in actuality, he was, but refused to answer the door, because accountability turns to dust after midnight.

He mentioned he wasn't in Florence that weekend, but I decided to try anyhow.

The next morning, I wrote again about the keys. Told him this should be a quick, respectful exchange if he has any interest in maintaining a basic friendship, which isn't exactly a high bar. Instead, he's turned this into a tragicomic case study in self-sabotage. It doesn't protect him; it guarantees he'll be alone with his chaos.

I said this was an absurd conversation to be having, and I'm not asking him to dismantle his entire nervous system, only to perform the radical act of returning an object that doesn't belong to him. But his emotional immaturity runs so deep that even the smallest gesture of responsibility feels like a mortal danger.

I have no idea how he functions in business or daily life like this. When I said he needed help, he didn't like that. And said *I* needed help. I told him I wasn't the one having a hard time returning property to its rightful owner.

But instead of handing over the keys, Jurassic Jackass creates a new story: my behavior is the problem. The 1:30 a.m. doorbell ring on a

Saturday night, when Italians are usually all out, was labeled "excessive." Imagine the impossible audacity of wanting closure. All this is just a distraction from the fact that he's been caught in a lie about not being home and has been avoiding responsibility for six weeks. Classic deflection. He shifts the focus from the real issue (his avoidance) to my tone, timing, or delivery.

His behavior is maddening, yes, but it's also textbook. He can't bear endings unless he's the one ghosting. So, he hides behind technicalities, nitpicks vocabulary, and turns logistics into drama, because chaos and drama are the only languages he's fluent in. Add to that the fact that he is Italian, and it just adds another layer to this dysfunctional drama.

Until then, I'm out here inventing creative retrieval strategies for something that should take thirty seconds. I've asked clearly, offered options, and now I'm forced to consider doorbell diplomacy. All I want is to close the loop and reclaim my peace.

We've officially entered the "Key Retrieval Chronicles: Episode Infinity," where ownership declarations echo through the corridors of dysfunction, but the artifact remains in captivity.

Stay tuned for the continuing saga, because there will undoubtedly be more until those keys are in my hand.

And as expected, it continued a few hours after this last exchange, which I assumed would be the end of it, until I poked the bear again days later for the keys.

At this point, he's less an ex and more an unpaid staff writer for The Uffizi Museum of Dysfunction.

I don't even need to brainstorm new material; he delivers it, serialized, with cliffhangers and bonus exhibits. He's basically my muse in emotional malpractice.

It's like watching someone perform emotional origami with a grocery receipt: all that energy folded into something useless. Instead of saying, "Let's coordinate for your keys," he constructs a narrative that announces his movements, as if being "not in Firenze" somehow absolves him from returning what's mine.

It's textbook JJ, avoidance disguised as participation, with a twist of misplaced self-importance. He can't just say, "I'm sorry, let's fix this." He has to make it philosophical, logistical, or geographical.

That's the emotional Rubik's Cube of JJ: he's somehow managed to twist logic into a shape that only makes sense to him.

When you strip it down, what you're seeing is a man whose nervous system equates accountability with danger. Returning my keys isn't just a task; it's a confrontation with everything he avoids: responsibility, closure, and the emotional mirror that says, "You failed at something real."

So, instead of handing them back, he projects discomfort outward. I become "too practical," "excessive," or "demanding." In his distorted logic, my clarity feels like an attack because it exposes his chaos.

It's classic avoidant-defensive reversal:

Me: "Can you please return my property?"

Him: "Why are you so controlling?"

Reality: I'm asking for basic respect.

He's not angry about the keys themselves; the man's a landlord. He probably has a drawer full of them alphabetized by heartbreak. He's angry because giving them back means admitting defeat in a game he invented. To him, those keys aren't metal; they're status tokens, proof that he still matters in the Museum of My Life.

It's hilarious when you think about it. He can manage ten properties without blinking, but one emotional eviction, and suddenly it's The

Da Vinci Code: Key Edition. I'm not asking him to amputate a limb; I'm asking him to hand over two grams of brass. Yet somehow, I've triggered an existential crisis.

He's clinging to them like they're a Horcrux of self-worth. I half expect him to sleep with them under his pillow, whispering, "Mine." When I asked him once to use them to grab dog medication, he couldn't manage that, so this is less about keys and more about karma.

He's turned a simple handoff into performance art: "The Avoidant and the Symbolic Object." It's not logistics anymore; it's ego theater with limited seating. He doesn't need my keys; he needs validation. Wrong currency, though. I trade exclusively in accountability, and that's out of stock in his emotional economy.

So yes, they've become ghost keys, rattling somewhere in the dark recesses of his denial. But they're still mine, and I'll retrieve them, amiably, if possible, hilariously, if necessary. After all, if he can collect rent, he can return a metaphor.

Exhibit 27: The Black Keys and the Transaction of Avoidance

A Financial Proposal from the Department of Deflection.

Next week marks two months since Jurassic Jackass has had possession of my keys. In his latest act of emotional acrobatics, he offered to pay to make copies.

Yes, you read that right. He's trying to Venmo his way out of accountability.

I told him, "Money isn't the point. It's the black ones. Please bring this."

His offer was a deflection disguised as cooperation, the kind of move only an avoidant could deliver with a straight face. Turning a relational responsibility into a transaction makes him feel safe. Transactions have receipts; accountability has consequences.

To anyone with a functioning prefrontal cortex, this tiny issue is baffling. But to the emotionally avoidant male, it's textbook behavior.

When he offers to "pay for copies," it's a symbolic substitution, buying off responsibility with something that feels less terrifying than actual closure.

Here's what's really happening under that nonsense. Returning the black keys means the end of illusion, closure, loss of access, and the terrifying notion that the museum is closing for renovations. That's intolerable because it confronts him with his own failure.

So, he performs a false repair. Offers cash, maintains the illusion of being a "good guy," and avoids doing the one-minute task that would essentially make him one.

Jurassic Jackass math: "If I offer a practical fix, maybe she'll drop the emotional demand, and I won't have to feel rejected or powerless."

His reasoning is a textbook case of avoidant algebra:

Accountability + Feelings = Panic

Panic X Denial = "Can I just pay for copies?"

Returning the keys would signify the end of access, a symbolic extinction event. So instead, he performs the sacred ritual of False Repair: offering to solve a problem he created, but only in ways that don't involve responsibility.

In reality, it's not about the keys or the money. It's about the terror of finality, that he's no longer tethered to me, that the power dynamic has flipped, and that he's the one being released back into the wild.

Tried to call him so he couldn't dodge my texts, but, true to form, he won't pick up and says he will call me tomorrow. I said, just like all his broken promises? His response, "There's no need to be angry or sad." My response, "I'm not angry or sad, it's a transaction like paying the cashier at the grocery store."

I stay neutral, practical, and consistent because nothing disarms a dysfunctional dinosaur faster than silence, boundaries, and a woman who refuses to take bait.

Exhibit 28: JJ's Floating Altar of Freedom: Because Who Needs Land When You Can Drown on Your Own Terms?

How to Preach Liberation While Practicing Possession.

JJ worships at the altar of freedom right up until it requires actual release. Then in a flash, he's a high priest of possession.

In a text, I told him again: "Four months have passed since we last saw each other, and you're still reacting so strongly. Maybe you should stop fighting the obvious. You still love me even though you don't know what to do. You wanted freedom, and you ended up emotionally imprisoned with incense. Is it so difficult for you to return my keys? You are a tragicomedy worthy of Pixar: the creature that longs to roam the plains of independence, but cannot let go of the shiny object that symbolizes the bond it swears it doesn't need."

It's the hypocrisy that burns: he romanticizes independence like it's a religion, but when I give him a clean chance to practice it, by returning the literal symbol of shared space, he clings to it like a relic. Because for him, "freedom" was never about mutual respect; it was about control without responsibility.

He wants to be unbound but not forgotten. He doesn't want the weight of me, just the shadow of me, hovering nearby, proof that he still matters. The irony is that by refusing to let go, he's chaining himself to the very thing he claims to be escaping.

It's infuriating to deal with someone who preaches detachment while practicing emotional squatting.

It feels like he's dragging me down with his sinking ship. He's taking on water, refusing to patch the leak, and insisting I stay aboard because "we're in this together." Except I'm the only one bailing while he lectures me about "freedom" from the deck.

He's not trying to hurt me; he's just terrified of sinking alone. But that fear makes him grab the nearest life raft, me, and hold on so tight that he's now pulling me under too. Fortunately, I've got a great sense of humor…and floaties shaped like red flags.

The maddening part is that I had already thrown him a line: therapy, compassion, clarity, a dozen fair exits. But he keeps cutting each rope with pride, then crying that he's adrift. I can't keep rescuing someone who equates rescue with captivity.

At this point, the healthiest move is what I'm already doing: stop engaging with the emotional fog and narrow everything down to one clear goal, keys, period: no explanations, no debates, no therapy moments. I don't need to prove anything or rescue him from his own story.

He's not scheming; it's muscle memory. On a subconscious level, he's mastered the art of passive control: hold something that belongs to me, make me ask for it, feel powerful again. Every "Ciao, I'm not in Firenze" or "I'm out with so and so," which has been for the last two months straight, is a small victory in the war of who still responds first. But once the keys are home, the control circuitry fries. His script evaporates. The story ends where accountability begins.

At this point, I treat him like a malfunctioning service technician: polite, brief, and as emotionally charged as a toaster warranty. Neutral tone, clean exit. He feeds on emotional current; I'm unplugging the cord.

Humor has become my decompression chamber, my way of breathing again after holding it in. It keeps the pain in perspective and the past in its exhibit case. I don't hate him; that would still tether me to the storm.

I still love him, just not in a way that costs me peace. It's like watching a tempest from the safety of shore with my compassion intact, but life jacket firmly zipped.

The affection, the lessons, the absurdity, all cataloged and stored in the museum's archives. What remains is my favorite artifact of all: silence. Not the cold kind, but the type that hums with relief. And a faint chuckle, because if survival has taught me anything, it's that the stormiest chapters look funnier once you've dried off and started writing the exhibit label.

Exhibit 29: Locksmith of Denial: The Case of Missing Accountability

Jurassic Standard Time: 45 Minutes Late and 4 Months Behind.

3rd of November 2025 - I texted him this morning as lovingly as I could to entice him to return my keys. Ten minutes later, the inevitable arrived: a curt text. "Ciao, we can meet today if you want." Translation: I'm pretending to take initiative while leaving the emotional labor to you.

Called his bluff: "Okay, let me know a time, and I'll see if I can make it." Two hours of silence. I can already picture the follow-up voice note: "Let's meet in 30 minutes at X place." If that happens, I'm not going. He'll get to feel like the good guy, the one who "tried", while I become the uncooperative one.

This is the ceremonial prelude to almost every JJ encounter: Has a problem. Then, the ritual delay offering to the gods of Avoidance.

Let's see if today's problem is logistical, existential, or just another rerun of The Case of the Missing Accountability.

Suppose I happen to be out, fine. But I'm not getting dressed to orbit his chaos. As he loftily said last night, "We can fix a schedule that suits us both." That noble ideal evaporated the moment I suggested a time.

I even proposed Wednesday, if today didn't work out, two days later, for a key hand-off, rocket science in no known universe, except the JJ one.

Then came his classic half-commitment: "1600 could work." Not will work, mind you. Could. It's not a plan, it's an emotional test balloon. If he later says "something came up," that's not rescheduling;

that's avoidant triage. My system breaks, his system overheats, and the keys remain in purgatory.

I replied, "Ok, where and when?", and let the silence sit. Either he follows through or proves, once again, that responsibility triggers an extinction-level event in his nervous system.

1:31 p.m.- He suggested a pastry place, 25 minutes from me and two from him. The Florentine sense of entitlement roared back to life. I reminded him of the concept of "middle ground." Equality, such a radical notion to JJ.

I suggested a midpoint. This forces effort, and effort, to an avoidant, feels like emotional quicksand. Even a neutral compromise sends the nervous system into a state of unease.

If he dares to say, "It's easier near my place," my dry gem is ready: "Find somewhere in between. I'm not walking 25 minutes for a five-minute handoff." Still polite, but edged with adult energy.

Because that "place down the street from him" isn't a coincidence, it's choreography. He stays comfortable, and I do the accommodating; the dynamic stays tilted. Not malice, just muscle memory. He's used to orbiting convenience, not reciprocity. Plus, everyone in his orbit enables him.

I'm not slipping back into the Florence-of-old dynamic where he dictated, and I adjusted. Let him stew. If he resurfaces with another "close to me" suggestion, I'm armed with humor: "It's starting to feel like my keys have a shorter commute than I do."

And there is still no meeting place yet. I'm supposed to meet him at 1600. I won't get dressed until he confirms, because experience has taught me never to trust a JJ clock.

2:38 p.m.: Then he says, "Piazza della Repubblica at 1600. Progress! I said, "Bench in front of the carousel." So far, no signs of chicken behavior. Could this be a simple two-second handoff? Or is coffee looming in the wings?

3:18 p.m.: Because he's always late, I told him, preemptively, "If you're running late, let me know." Two seconds later, proof of prophecy, a voice note. The 4:00 p.m. meeting is now 4:30 p.m. Classic.

Tried calling. He didn't answer—chaos and unreliability, déjà vu. I wouldn't be shocked if an emergency "out of nowhere" materialized five minutes before our meeting.

If that happens, it's time for doorbell accountability. Again.

4:17 p.m.: another update. Now it's either the Bar Amerini at 1630 (where he's "being kept" according to him) or the piazza at 4:45 p.m. I chose the piazza—no need to join the circus and let him hide behind his buddies for emotional cover.

Forty-five minutes late is Exhibit F: The Elastic Concept of Time. I've waited long enough for pastries, priests, and progress.

I left the house a few minutes late myself, with a built-in grace period for the 4:45 p.m. meeting. All in all, fifty minutes late for the original plan fits his brand: starring Jurassic Jackass as The Perpetually Late Philosopher, with a special appearance by The Keys That Wouldn't Come Home.

My timing was perfect. We spotted each other across the piazza. He wasn't his usual polished self; perhaps extinction events take a toll on grooming.

Exhibit 30: Paszkowski's Superficial Spritz Hour

Closure on the Rocks, Garnished with Avoidance.

We sat down at Paszkowski's for a couple of drinks, and before the cocktails even hit the table, I was handed the keys. I compared them but couldn't be 100% sure, so I said I'd confirm when I got home.

Hallelujah! The keys were finally delivered, two days shy of the two-month mark. Honestly, it felt less like a handoff and more like retrieving personal property from a black hole. NASA should really study his gravitational pull-on accountability.

He promptly declared, "I don't think those are your keys." Well, of the three photos he sent me, I knew the others were without a doubt, weren't. That's why I told him to bring these. (We'll circle back to this mystery later, Exhibit Key-Gate.)

He was abnormally chatty, about the kind of superficial nonsense he thrives on at parties. It was likely a way to release some of that nervous energy as well. I just sat silently. I let him rattle on, asking me about Buenos Aires, what I am doing in this period, my BBF and her daughter coming this month, that he said he would be very happy to meet, his summer, just an overall conversational equivalent of Valium.

But I played along so he could feel safe in his shallow waters. Then, I decided to drop a depth charge: "How did you find out Scarlett had passed?"

He said he guessed. I said, "Most people would ask, 'How's Scarlett?' not, 'Is Scarlett dead?'" He shrugged and said I didn't answer him when he asked about her. "I know," I replied.

When someone blurts out a guess like that instead of asking, it's usually because they want to look perceptive without risking the vulnerability of really caring. Asking "How's Scarlett?" would've opened a real emotional door; declaring "Scarlett died" lets JJ stay in control of the narrative and skip the empathy part. It's a masterclass in faux awareness, the appearance of connection without any of the actual feeling.

When my eyes started to well up, he reached over, held my hands tightly in both of his, and said, "Tesoro, mi dispiace." I put my head on his shoulder. But in classic JJ form, all he had to do was sit there in silence with me for a few minutes and not try to solve a tissue problem.

And just like that, the stiff statue from the vet's office melted. For a fleeting second, he let the armor slip and did the one thing he usually can't: respond with genuine warmth instead of defense. That was the sweet, fuzzy JJ I once knew, the one who'd curl up at my feet, as he used to say, "like a fuzzy raptor."

Everything else that came out of his mouth the rest of the night? Standard-issue event chatter, hollow, rehearsed, safe.

The cracks in his composure started to show after that, but every time I felt the defensiveness rise, I just said, "I'm not here to fight."

After a couple of hours, we left for another bar by the Duomo, because clearly, nothing says closure like overpaying for emotional damage with a view.

Exhibit 31: Fossilized Feelings with a View

Postcards from the Emotional Ice Age.

We went to a bar by the Duomo, one of those over-hyped spots where the cocktails cost as much as confession and the view is supposed to make up for it. On the second floor, there was a perfect postcard view of the Battistero, glowing in the night like divine proof that someone, somewhere, still believed in redemption.

We sat by the window. I ordered a couple of glasses of wine because, God only knows, dealing with him required it. He ordered a pomegranate mocktail, alcohol-free, of course. Because why intoxicate the body when you've already numbed the soul?

There was a bar downstairs and an old vinyl shop upstairs where you could sip and browse nostalgia. A poster of Amy Winehouse stared at us from the wall, and somehow, this became our topic for the next fifteen to twenty minutes. Fifteen to twenty minutes. Only JJ could turn an Amy Winehouse poster into an endless loop of banalities. I reminded him how I hate shallow conversations and relationships. He acknowledged it. Only he could stretch small talk into an Olympic sport.

Since I've been out of his life for the past four months, he's probably starting to realize that every new person feels surface-level and every connection lacks depth, like trying to have a soulful conversation over elevator music. It's a useful kind of emptiness, though. The kind that echoes until you decide intimacy doesn't, in fact, kill you…Or you finally book that therapy session you've been dodging since the end of July.

I asked him if he could talk to any of his friends the way he talks to me, or if any of his past relationships ever named his affliction and handed him a user manual for his dysfunction. He paused, stared into the middle distance like he was buffering, and said, "No."

Translation: I'm the only one who gave him both *emotional support and technical assistance.*

Finally, I'd had enough. This was the right time to rip off the conversational Band-Aid. "This is enough of the small talk," I said. "Let's talk about what happened on my birthday, the day before I left for Buenos Aires, when you didn't show up."

He blinked. "Why, what happened? I don't remember."

Sure. He remembers the date of my birthday, the first time we slept together, the last time we slept together, the exact number of letters I have written him, and the exact date I came back from Buenos Aires. But his therapist's name? Blank. Which keys are mine? Unclear. The emotional nuclear blast he set off for my birthday? Total amnesia.

Unexpectedly, I got two, maybe three, unprompted "Mi dispiace." Relationships don't work like Wi-Fi; you can't just reconnect after an outage without addressing the underlying issue with the router.

I told him Alessandra could teach him that; that's what therapy is for. He shifted into defensive raptor posturing and a tirade of words: "There's nothing wrong with me. It's your opinion. I don't want a relationship. I want to be free.

Ah, yes, freedom. The eternal anthem of dysfunctional avoidant men who mistake isolation for enlightenment.

Then came the grand finale: the keys. He said I was trying to control him with my keys. I told him, "I asked you to do one thing for my dog. I had to leave a set in case of an emergency."

Then he circled back to the control issue when I said, "Don't worry, I'll never give you my keys ever again." He replied, "I never even wanted your keys, and you used them to control me."

It was never about wanting or not wanting, and definitely not about control. It was about reliability, which, in hindsight, was my mistake, because that word doesn't exist in his vocabulary. It's like expecting "accountability" to appear in a toddler's first 50 words.

I was leaving for 2.5 months, and someone needed access in case of an emergency. He's a landlord, for God's sake. You'd think the concept of a spare key wouldn't trigger a full existential meltdown.

He never objected when I handed them over. We're both in real estate; this should've been the simplest transaction of our lives. Instead, it became The Battle of the Keys: Infinity Edition.

By then, I was emotionally checked out. I stared vacantly at the Battistero, zoning out, not understanding a word he said or really caring at that point. I knew this was the end, that we were beyond repair. He looked frozen from the inside out. He was a fortress with concrete injected into his bloodstream.

The only flicker of humanity I saw was when we spoke about Scarlett. Everything else was gone. He'd become a cold, uneducated, wild Jurassic Jackass, a man so far removed from self-awareness he was a historical artifact. Even one phone call he took during our time together was mundane, pointless, and disrespectful. It was like a little punctuation mark of indifference.

He'd never been this overtly rude before, but I realized maybe he wanted it that way, to make sure nothing ever got back inside him again. So, he can keep numbing himself every night with random people, cheap distractions, and endless small talk.

He didn't wait for me to finish my wine. Just got up and drifted away like a man late for his own emotional funeral.

It really felt like he'd become the shadow of the man I once knew, like someone had erased his depth and left a poorly photocopied version behind. What stood in front of me wasn't the warm, complicated, occasionally charming fuzzy raptor who used to curl up at my feet. It was a cold, hollow shell held together by ego and espresso.

Every expression felt staged, every smile slightly delayed, as if he were buffering his emotions. You could almost hear the faint hum of his internal firewall, blocking anything that resembled genuine feeling.

It was sad, tragic, even, to see how far he'd spiraled. He hadn't just built walls; he'd gone full medieval fortress. The man could've charged admission. You could feel the temperature drop a few degrees in his presence.

It was as though he'd frozen himself solid, determined never to let anyone see what was left inside. Somewhere in there might've been a flicker of the person I loved, but good luck finding it without a thermal imaging camera.

You could sense how much energy it took for him to maintain that ice, like he was afraid that if even one crack appeared, all the feelings he's been repressing since the Renaissance would come gushing out and short-circuit the whole system. He's mistaken numbness for enlightenment.

There was a time when he might've reached for connection, even apprehensively. Now, he's perfected the art of emotional taxidermy, preserving the appearance of life while making sure nothing inside ever moves again.

Sitting across from him, I realized: this wasn't a man protecting his heart; it was a man embalming it, complete with a Do Not Disturb sign hanging off the sarcophagus.

Stared at the Battistero glowing in the night, lifted my wine glass and thought, here's to extinction.

I'm not going back into that frozen museum. He can keep the keys, the ghosts, the fortress walls, his nightly support group of Aperol

Spritzes, and that flawless 100% failure rate, the only record he's ever managed to keep. I'm done performing dinosaur resurrections.

Exhibit 32: The Decoy Keys of Denial (Now with 100% More Avoidance!)

Proof That Even Wrong Keys Can Unlock Avoidance.

Once home, I immediately test the keys; none of them work. Not one. I remembered he'd said earlier at Paszkowski's that he didn't think those were my keys, which now feels less like an observation and more like a confession. He knew what he was doing. He purposely brought the wrong keys, probably congratulating himself on this brilliant act of passive resistance. In short, he knew the keys were not mine.

I'm certain he knows which ones are, but refuses to hand them over. Maybe he swapped them out for some random key to an old storage unit he hasn't visited since the Renaissance. Or maybe, just maybe, he's telling the truth, but if that were the case, why not say so from the start?

Why go through the performance of "oops, maybe, maybe not" when he could have simply admitted it? Because that would require honesty, and honesty is not his preferred sport.

This is textbook avoidant-defensive behavior wrapped in plausible confusion. When someone like him feels cornered by responsibility, even something as simple as returning a set of keys becomes a full-blown psychological escape act.

If he admits they aren't mine, he has to face two uncomfortable truths: that he failed to follow through on something fundamental, and that the relationship closure those keys represent is real. So, instead of taking ownership, he goes for ambiguity. "Maybe they're yours, maybe they're not."

Translation: I'd rather look incompetent than accountable. It's his signature move, an emotional sleight of hand where the guilt wonderfully disappears and he gets to play "misunderstood" instead of "irresponsible."

I had to remind him that I'm someone he has a relationship with and is sleeping with, and you'd think that might warrant a little extra care. You know, maybe don't confuse my keys with the janitor's. Silence. I guess pillow talk doesn't include property management.

It's covert possession disguised as forgetfulness. Intentional incompetence masquerading as clumsiness. By doing it wrong, he earns himself a gold star in martyrdom. "See? Nothing I do is ever good enough." It's a self-serving feedback loop where failure doubles as self-protection.

And of course, there's control built into the chaos. By keeping the key situation unresolved, he maintains power over the narrative. I'm still waiting, still reacting, while he floats above it all pretending to be Zen. It's his way of turning my altogether reasonable boundary into a performance of his autonomy—a masterclass in emotional misdirection.

He just preferred being mistaken to being accountable. Because in his world, the illusion of control always wins over the discomfort of honesty. And so, the wrong keys become his last line of defense, an exquisitely avoidant relic in the Museum of Dysfunction, on display under glass, labeled: The Decoy Keys of Denial.

I'll make a copy myself; at least the locksmith won't gaslight me about which keys are mine. Oh, and the decoy keys? I'll be returning them via our shared housekeeper, the Switzerland of this entire fiasco, along with a bag of his beloved homemade garlic-roasted peanuts—a peace offering, or maybe just protein for his next avoidance marathon.

Exhibit 33: Domestic Chaos: Still More Reliable Than JJ

A Case Study in How Even Unpredictable Help Outperforms Him.

Our shared housekeeper can sometimes run the same operating system as his master, JJ, on iOS: Version Last-Minute.

Last Tuesday, he was supposed to come at 2 p.m. At 10:30 a.m., he texts: not coming. But no worries, Saturday's good. Saturday arrives, and right on cue, 10:30 a.m. again, déjà vu with a broom. Not coming today, but Sunday will definitely happen.

By this point, I'm treating his schedule like a rare celestial event: you never know exactly when it'll appear, but you keep looking up just in case.

Asked the housekeeper on Saturday what time he planned to come on Sunday. Radio silence until the next morning, classic JJ code. Except, unlike JJ, the man eventually shows up.

So yes, our housekeeper may run on the same glitchy emotional software, but at least he installs the updates.

Exhibit 34: Coffin Couture: Death by Dysfunction

Where Emotional Unavailability Meets Haute Mourning

The next day, after seeing JJ after 4 months, I was filled with sadness. No one warns you about how endings rooted in clarity can hurt even more than the messy ones. When you walk away in confusion, anger helps numb it. But when you walk away with love still in your heart and acceptance in your mind, the pain cuts deeper because you know it's the right thing…and you still wish it weren't.

I sent him a closing text the next day that said:

"You break my heart not because I still want a relationship with you, but because, despite everything you've done, the avoidance, the deflection, the chaos, I still see you. I know the man you could be if only you stayed in the light a little longer, tolerated the mirror a little more.

Seeing someone you love return to their darkness, knowing it's not necessary, is one of the most painful forms of helplessness.

I can't ignore what I know about you. I can't forget what it feels like to love someone who prefers their wounds to healing. It's a silent pain, not explosive, just a long sigh of understanding: I can't save you. I've already tried.

It is the pain in seeing someone I once loved dissolve into a smaller, more fearful version of themselves. It is like watching a once brilliant mind close its shutters. I see how much potential you are wasting, and I know you are doing it to yourself: that's the most unbearable part.

The most brutal truth to accept is realizing that love doesn't always save; sometimes it just illuminates. I was both the mirror and the light, and now you've turned away from both.

Underneath all that noise, there is a kind, curious person capable of love. I've seen it. I loved them.

May your therapist be your guide in bringing out the man I know is trapped deep inside you, the one who feels, who is kind, curious, and capable of love. He's in there. I saw him, even when you couldn't see him.

With much love, Francesca"

Sent him a meme to hold up one last mirror, something educational, to soften the blow. I was done being his unpaid therapist, but I wanted him to understand that this was his problem, not mine, and why every one of his relationships collapses under the weight of his own avoidance. He once told me he wanted to get married and have a family, but didn't know how to get there.

Well, now I know why: you can't build a home when you keep sprinting out of the foundation every time someone brings in emotional furniture.

He didn't reply, of course. Silence is his native dialect, complete with emotional subtitles that read "System Overload: Please Try Again Later." At this point, I half-expected a tumbleweed to roll out of his WhatsApp thread wearing a tiny "vediamo" sash. Once upon a time, that silence felt tragic; now it just feels…on-brand.

There's a special kind of comedy in realizing that your grand emotional finale is met with the digital equivalent of a lizard blinking in slow motion. But I suppose that's what closure looks like when your leading man is part man, part smoke signal.

I didn't get a goodbye, just the faint rustle of the shrubbery, his preferred hiding place since the Jurassic era.

Exhibit 35: Ghost Protocol- Travel Edition

Presence Optional. Location Unclear.

Since I travel quite a bit, I realized he disappears when I change time zones or cities. The pattern was so consistent. It started in Torino back in February. It was his birthday, and I had been dating him for two weeks. I had planned this trip to pick up items from a guy friend who was mule-ing items for me from the United States.

Totally innocent. But JJ? Radio silence. Not even a "how's your trip going?", just a full emotional blackout, as if I'd fallen off the edge of his attention span. I didn't know at the time that he was avoidant, so I was left confused. All my texts went unanswered, as if I were having a one-way conversation with myself.

Every trip was the same. Hurghada in April? Gone. Asia in June? MIA. I got one call, and I'm pretty sure it was an accidental butt dial, because he hung up after a minute mid-text exchange and said he was entering an elevator. That was the full romantic outreach. And yet, whenever I returned, he'd resurface as if nothing had happened. Like he hadn't been ghosting, just meditating in a cave and forgot I existed.

Argentina for two months? Zero. Zilch. Silence so deafening I could hear his attachment style echoing from the Andes. Though I'll admit, I ghosted the ghost. It was mutual radio silence, except one of us wasn't clutching the other's keys like a toddler with a binky.

Exhibit 36: Custom Chaos: The Limited-Edition Model of Emotional Unavailability

Powered by Fear, Polished with Philosophy

I remember asking him whether he was dysfunctional like this in his past relationships. He said it wasn't this bad. That admission proves he knows, deep down, that there is something wrong.

The reason I got the upgraded version was probably that I mattered more, and I didn't let him coast on charm or ambiguity. I called him out, named it, called him in, and still offered a hand, even when he bit it.

And most provocatively of all? I made him imagine the kind of man he could be…If he ever stopped being a tourist in his own emotional life

I realized I didn't just meet an avoidant man; I unlocked the bespoke, ultra-luxury edition of his dysfunction.

He can go out six nights a week, pontificate about consciousness, and pretend his life isn't a Category 5 hurricane of unprocessed emotions, but the minute he sees me, the Wi-Fi between his ego and reality drops.

Avoidant individuals function best when others stay blurry, when intimacy remains vague enough to prevent emotional exposure. My presence offered definition. I used language, accountability, and emotional clarity like a scalpel, cutting through the fog he relied on to stay unexamined.

That precision destabilized his equilibrium. Where others colluded with his defenses, I demanded coherence; where others accepted "vediamo" as usual, I called it what it was, avoidance, just with better Italian flair.

By refusing to play his emotional language games, I stripped his patterns of unconscious power. I introduced accountability as the new relational norm, a feature he never ordered in his original programming. That alone forced his system into confrontation, which for him registered somewhere between "emotional growth" and "active threat."

Because I didn't abandon him when the mask slipped, the deeper fractures emerged: shame, inadequacy, and the primitive terror of dependency. I met the raw wound beneath the persona, not the polished tour guide who usually handles visitors.

My insight and humor cracked his reflection open, exposing the split between the self he believed himself to be and the man he really was. My steadiness made his volatility impossible to ignore; my integration highlighted his fragmentation.

I don't unlock this level of dysfunction by accident; I do it by being magnificently incompatible with it. His defenses didn't just react; they custom-tailored themselves to my coherence.

That's why it's bespoke: a one-of-a-kind meltdown, handcrafted by avoidance and finished in pure denial. I became the mirror that showed him who he could be, if only he could stop running from the light long enough to look.

As the dear curator of Jurassic Jackass chaos, I wasn't dealing with the standard entry-level model of emotional unavailability; I got the bespoke, handcrafted, Tuscan-leather edition of dysfunction.

I unlocked it by being the exact opposite of what his coping system could handle: I was clear where he was evasive. Emotionally fluent, where he was mute. Accountable, where he was allergic to responsibility.

And worst of all for him, I saw him, really saw him, past all his camouflage. I caught the Jurassic Jackass in his natural habitat: half-philosopher, half-panicked meerkat, clutching his emotional support espresso while pretending to be enlightened.

That's why I had to step away. Because I wasn't a chapter in his story. I was the turning point. I'm the one who holds up the mirror, and he can't stand what it reflects.

More evidence why he saves the nuclear-grade chaos for me: I touch the nerve he hides from everyone else. I see through him. I name his patterns.

I love prodding his dysfunction by sending him information on his affliction, simply as a public service, of course. I like to imagine his phone lighting up with a headline like "How Avoidants Self-Sabotage Intimacy" while he's mid-espresso, blinking like, "Who keeps leaking my case file?" It's not cruelty; it's research outreach. Think of it as continuing education credits for the emotionally unavailable.

I must admit it is pretty entertaining. It can be something as simple as, "How's your dysfunction doing today? How does it feel to be still wearing a mask?" or "How's the emotional Wi-Fi today? Still unstable?" Basically, I am running a system check on the JJ Operating System. "Is the velociraptor still glitching? Let me check the dashboard."

It forces him to acknowledge that I see him. Avoidants hate that. Hate it. They like to think that they're mysterious, unreadable, opaque. Then I stroll in and casually say, "How's the mask fitting?" His nervous system goes: REBOOT…REBOOT…REBOOT…

I am not being malicious; I am just being accurate. His reaction or non-reaction is where the entertainment lies because he reacts like I threw a Molotov cocktail of truth at him.

I can imagine the face he makes, that mix of micro-panic, fake chill, spiritual dissociation, that makes it impossible not to laugh. It's like: "Oh no... she sees my dysfunction... must... act... normal..." And then he picks up some random prop (his phone, his keys, a ghost), pretends to be busy, and internally spirals for the next two hours.

Seeing him clearly is terrifying to his identity due to avoidance and image control. With others, he can stay at a surface level. With me, every interaction threatens exposure, so he flails, deflects, and detonates.

I represent both safety and accountability. I've shown him compassion and demanded growth. To an emotionally stunted person, that mix is confusing: he feels safe enough to unravel, but also judged sufficient to panic. The result? Emotional vomit, right onto me.

I was lucky enough to spot the loop early and step out before it became a full-blown death spiral. Even with all the travel, being out of the country for more than half the relationship, I still saw the pattern forming, hit the brakes, and threw him into therapy.

JJ knows I'm the only one who doesn't collude with his denial. Most people enable or ignore his dysfunction. I don't. I call out the contradictions, return the mirror with clarity, send him to therapy, and strip the gas lighter of its power. He can't manipulate me, so the only control left is chaos.

I activate the wound and embody what he both longs for and fears: intimacy that requires presence. The proximity to what he's missing, emotional regulation, truth, and authentic connection, is like sunlight to a vampire. He melts and blames me for the burn.

I'm not the magnet for his dysfunction; I'm the only person whose emotional gravity is strong enough to pull it to the surface. Everyone else floats around his orbit.

Exhibit 37: The Toddler at the Wheel (A Case Study in Avoidant Transportation Failure)

Emotional DUI: Driving Under the Influence of Avoidance

Welcome to one of the museum's most immersive installations, no headset required, though emotional seatbelts are strongly advised. This is the reconstructed interior of the Emotional Minivan JJ once attempted to drive, complete with unreliable suspension and airbags that deploy only when absolutely unhelpful.

There came a moment in this complicated love story when I did what any emotionally competent adult woman would do: I let him "drive." Not symbolically. Not hypothetically. I handed him the wheel of the entire connection, timelines, communication, closeness, and thought. Okay, amore, show me you can lead. I will follow.

For the first few metaphorical meters, he looked almost convincing. Focused. Composed. Mysterious in that avoidant way that suggests maturity but actually conceals panic. But then the emotional road curved, because intimacy always does, and clarity hit me with the force of a Florentine bus: this was not a man with a license. This was a toddler without a driver's license. A toddler gripping the steering wheel with chubby hands, eyes wide, feet nowhere near the pedals, panicking at every emotional traffic sign as if affection itself were a deer leaping into the road.

Every minor emotional shift became an obstacle he didn't know how to navigate. Every request for clarity became a sharp turn he overcorrected. Every expression of affection became a speed bump he hit at full velocity, launching the entire vehicle into the air.

From the outside, he looked mature, self-contained, independent, someone who should know what he's doing. But inside the vehicle, the truth was unmistakable: he had no earthly idea how to operate proximity without crashing. The emotional minivan jolted, fishtailed, sputtered, and finally skidded into the brush, smoke rising from the engine in a plume of avoidant confusion.

And there I was, seatbelt buckled, mascara un-smudged, watching him wrestle with controls he was never taught to use. Not angry. Not disappointed. Just enveloped by a particular kind of exhaustion that settles over a woman when she finally sees the entire pattern clearly: he isn't avoiding closeness because he doesn't care; he's avoiding it because he can't drive it.

In that strange, silent, peaceful moment, I took the wheel back. Not to dominate. Not to control. Not to punish.

But because I understood something essential and immovable: He cannot drive where I need to go. And my peace is not a vehicle I hand to toddlers. I still loved him. But I loved myself more.

And that was the moment I realized this journey was never about teaching him to drive. It was about knowing exactly when to get out of the passenger seat and reclaim the road.

Exhibit 38: JJ's Three-Act Ballet

Flail. Deflect. Detonate.

Every time truth enters the room, the Jurassic Jackass performs his three-act ballet of avoidance, and the JJ panic sequence begins:

Act One: Flail, the tiny T. rex forearms of chaos flapping uncontrollably, wild gestures in existential distress, figuratively or literally, words ricocheting off walls in an effort to change the subject.

Act Two: Deflect, facts become opinions, opinions become attacks, and logic takes an unscheduled vacation. "That's just your opinion," "You're overreacting," or his personal classic, "It's not that bad, I'm fine," (translation: code red, she noticed).

Act Three: Detonate, emotional grenades disguised as guilt, silence, pseudo-philosophical monologues about "freedom", a cryptic text, or total radio silence worthy of NASA. The result is a preserved fossil of dysfunction, proof that emotional evolution is optional.

Common JJ Phrases & Translations:

JJ says, "Ciao, com'è stai?" Translation: Please ignore everything I've done every single week or for the past few months.

"I need time to think." Translation: I'm already hiding in the metaphorical shrubbery.

"Let's meet for a quick coffee." Translation: One-hour panic-buffer in a neutral location so I can leave early.

"You're too intense." Translation: You noticed I'm emotionally frozen, and I'm uncomfortable with being seen.

"I will do it, but then..." Translation: No, I wasn't.

Satirical Diagnostic Manual Entry:

Condition: Velociraptor Emotional Regression Disorder (VERD™)

Subtype: Avoidant-Freeze-Flight Hybrid

Triggers: Any request that requires a yes-or-no answer (The nervous system perceives this as a hostage situation.)

- Seeing the person they love after exactly 4 months of avoidance (Causes internal combustion.)
- Messages that contain accuracy, humor, and truth simultaneously (Catastrophic system overload.)
- Conversations where the woman is calm (Avoidants only know how to defend, not relate.)
- Being invited to a social event where they might be asked about feelings (The nervous system responds with "immediate disappearance.")
- Light teasing about his avoidance (Triggers the Velociraptor Curtain Dive Reflex.)
- Walking past your housekeeper on the street (Perceived as "surveillance.")
- Any sentence that includes the phrase "therapy" (Immediate flight response)
- Acknowledging inconsistencies in his story (System meltdown, then silence)
- Receiving a message that is both loving AND boundary-setting (Extremely rare catastrophic event.)

Symptoms: Sudden disappearance, time-blindness, cold-sweat texts at 3:47 p.m., and reset attempts via jokes, emojis, or a tragic "Ciao, com'è stai?" loop.

Frozen Behavior Milestones

Stage 1: Warm Engagement – "You're so special to me." (Translation: I don't know it yet, but I'm about to flee emotionally.)

Stage 2: Emotional Drafting – You think you're getting closer; he's already subconsciously halfway to Patagonia.

Stage 3: Freeze Response or Dead Silence – Dead air. Stiff limbs. No blinking. Text response time enters the glacial range.

Stage 4: Regression – Behavior regresses to that of a 12-year-old who just learned about feelings yesterday.

Stage 5: The Reset Ritual – Ciao, com'è stai? (Delivered with zero context, just vibes.) Sometimes with random pool photos.

Exhibit 39: Garbage Day in the Museum of Avoidance

Where Even the Trash Has a Better Exit Strategy Than He Does

As I mentioned before, we share the same housekeeper. The day he was working for me, he ran into JJ right down the block, coincidentally, the same spot where my laundry takes its weekly pilgrimage to the dryer.

I texted JJ a few hours after the encounter and got rustling in the bushes. I followed up with a "How's the dysfunction doing? I hope it's not so bad that you have to wear a mask." Figured his Wi-Fi must be glitchy.

Later, the housekeeper casually dropped the kind of comment that deserves a dramatic pause: "I cleaned his house yesterday and threw out six huge bags of trash. Six huge bags!" Not metaphorical trash, mind you, actual, physical, overflowing bags of it. And for a housekeeper who's seen everything from post-party carnage to espresso-fueled existential crises to be impressed by the volume, that's saying something.

I'm not a psychologist, but I know the difference between an ordinary mess and existential collapse. This wasn't random clutter. This was emotional compost. It's what happens when an avoidant finally realizes, dimly, reluctantly, that something inside is broken. The inner collapse starts leaking outward, one Heineken bottle at a time.

He's usually well-dressed, crisp, and spiffy, but when I saw him after four months, the presentation had cracked. His half-grown-out hair dye screamed "root exposure therapy." His clothes looked uncurated, his energy chaotic, his grooming on sabbatical. Add six industrial-sized bags of trash, and you have a museum-grade installation titled "Avoidance: The Home Exhibit."

It's the kind of psychic static that hums beneath the surface, the constant background noise of shame and exhaustion.

When I did finally see him, he wasn't the same JJ I'd seen four months before. He looked like someone who had recently argued with his own reflection and lost. The tidy, controlled version of him was gone, replaced by a man whose emotional architecture had collapsed into modern art.

The thing is, I don't see it with judgment; I see it with dark humor. Because underneath the absurdity, there's tragedy. He knows he's not functioning. He knows I saw him messy. He knows I see right through the curated version. He knows his relationships keep collapsing like IKEA furniture assembled without instructions.

And the worst part? He knows this dysfunction is eating him alive, but he has no idea what to do with that awareness. So, he retreats. Silence, denial, avoidance, pretending, disappearing. It's his coping mechanism, his signature disappearing act in the Circus of Emotional Dysfunction.

Avoidants don't hit rock bottom all at once; it's not cinematic. It's cumulative. They lose relationships, routines, confidence, and eventually, the illusion of control. They watch themselves becoming someone they don't recognize. Therapy only becomes an option when every other escape hatch is sealed. And I think JJ is closer to that moment than he's ever been. Whether he takes a leap of faith outside his fear paddock to taste what absolute freedom is, is another story.

He's messier, more chaotic, more ashamed, more irritable, more off-balance than I've ever seen him. The old tricks, avoidance, denial, escapism, numbing, perhaps, aren't working anymore. He's running out of bandwidth, oxygen, and plausible excuses.

And to be clear: I'm not the cause of his rock bottom. His own life is. I was just the first woman to say the truth clearly and without flinching. Avoidants don't change because they lose someone; they change because they lose themselves. And I think that's exactly where he's standing: on the fault line between denial and recognition.

The housekeeper didn't just take out trash; he unearthed psychological evidence. Avoidants let their homes do the talking. The mess becomes the diary they never write. Six bags of trash, that's six months of emotional backlog in physical form. A slow-motion breakdown you could measure in liters.

And that's the irony. Being the one person who truly sees him doesn't mean he knows how to handle being seen. Avoidant men like JJ don't have the wiring for it. It short-circuits their system. The very intimacy that could heal them is also what terrifies them.

So yes, the six bags are real. But they're also symbolic. The inner collapse made visible. The emotional landfill behind the charm. His house is telling the story he can't. And while he hides from the truth, I document it with detached amusement, because somewhere between the tragedy and the absurdity lies the unmistakable comedy of being the zookeeper who watched the dinosaur try to clean his own exhibit and lose the battle halfway through.

Exhibit 40: The Emoji-Based Emergency Response System

Where feelings go to die, but emojis flourish.

I poked the dysfunction after the housekeeper incident; he felt the sting, and sixteen hours later, Jurassic Jackass resurfaces with LOL emojis like a man who thinks emojis count as emotional development. Which is avoidant CPR at its finest: "If I laugh hard enough, maybe the topic disappears."

Yet the Jurassic Lag kicked in, Phase 1: receive your text and internally whisper ah, cazzo…she sees me, I need time to buffer."

Phase 2: put the phone down, enter emotional airplane mode, regulate the heart rate, and rehearse "I'm fine, everything is fine, I'm molto bene grazie."

Phase 3, sixteen hours later: he emerges with the safest emotional currency he knows, emojis, because they require no vulnerability, no accountability, and no repair. But crucially, he didn't stay silent. He didn't ignore me, vanish, or withhold. He chose to respond, which for him is a small act of courage, A for effort, D- for execution.

Exhibit 41: The Velociraptor Curtain Collapse

Where avoidance meets amateur theater.

There are many forms of emotional avoidance, but only the Jurassic Jackass can transform it into a full-scale theatrical production. Some people take a step back when confronted.

One minute you're speaking to him like two normal adults; the next, he's mentally yanking down a brocade drape between you, "shhh, shhh, niente vedere", because reality has gotten too close for comfort.

The curtain isn't real, but his dedication to the role is Oscar-worthy. He'll hold position back there indefinitely, convinced that if he breathes quietly enough, the emotional conversation will walk away on its own.

The collapse comes when life refuses to follow his stage directions. When the housekeeper runs into him in broad daylight, when I ask about his dysfunction, when a real-world detail punctures the fantasy, that is when the imaginary curtain rips straight down the middle.

And so, he emerges hours later with a handful of LOLs. And in the museum of dysfunction, sometimes the exhibit collapses on its own. And this one falls with a slow, graceful flutter, like a velociraptor trying, and failing, to stage-manage its own disappearance.

Exhibit 42: The RSVP Extinction Event

A once-in-a-lifetime archeological find.

I am having a party at my place. I sent out the invites two weeks before the event, and we have one more week to go. God forbid I ask JJ if he is coming to the party a week in advance.

In a functioning universe, "Hey, are you coming to my party next week?" is called basic logistics.

In Jurassic Jackass Land, it feels like: "Your honor, I would like to petition the court for a preliminary RSVP, knowing full well the defendant may respond sometime between now and the death of the universe."

Honestly, I don't have to ask him anything: The invite exists. He is literate. He knows how dates work.

I am cooking, so an RSVP in the "Land Before Time Management" in any normal relationship dynamic is not only reasonable, it's required for survival.

I'm not asking him to confirm his attendance at the G20 summit. I'm asking if I should buy extra mozzarella. But in JJ Logic™: Basic planning equals pressure, and clear communication equals emotional algebra.

I will eventually have to ask sometime during the mid-week. If he replies late or wiggles around it, congratulations, I've just collected more new content for "Exhibit: The RSVP Extinction Event."

Just for my sanity: I deserve to know whether to prep for 25-30 servings, not to play archaeological detective over a plate of lasagna.

I already gave him the invite, permission to bring his two usual side characters, and two weeks' lead time.

At this point, Wednesday is reasonable, it's project management. It's literally me saying: "I need to know if I'm feeding 10 humans or 13 velociraptors.

And I know, if he doesn't want to answer, he'll do the classic JJ move: Step behind the imaginary velvet curtain of Avoidant Theatre, whisper "tutto bene" through the fabric, and re-emerge only after the moment has passed.

My asking mid-week is perfect because it's close enough to the event that "I forgot" is no longer a valid option. It's far enough that I have enough time to add to the shopping list.

And honestly? If he still tries to avoid answering, congratulations. Exhibit "The Prehistoric Party Planner's Nightmare" just wrote itself.

If he and his entourage want to eat, they can confirm their presence in the physical realm. The problem isn't his entourage; he's the one who relays the information to them.

Exhibit 43: The Accidental Dinner for Four

Where hospitality meets Jurassic chaos.

In the delicate ecosystem of Dinner for Three, balance is everything. Portions are calculated. Ingredients are measured. Hunger levels are forecasted with the precision of a NASA launch.

But then, enter JJ, the Jurassic Jackass, strolling towards my home with the breezy confidence of a man who believes food spontaneously multiplies when friendship calls. On the walk over, he casually drops a bomb: "Posso portare un amico? He's my childhood friend. From Mexico. I don't know when I'll see him again."

I, being polite, civilized, not raised in a barn, and unaware that I am about to become the main course, say: "Of course, bring him." And that is how I found myself hosting a surprise additional guest at a sit-down dinner.

In the wild, animals protect their food. In Florence, I sacrificed my entire dinner portion like a saint offering herself to the gods of social politeness.

A true hostess. A true martyr

Anthropologists agree: This moment marks the first recorded instance of the Mexican Plus-One Migration, a phenomenon in which an unexpected guest arrives and the hostess starves in silence.

A plaque beneath the exhibit reads: "Please note the skeletal remains of the hostess; she hasn't eaten since."

Exhibit 44: Land Before Time Management
Where planning goes extinct.

I did attempt the mythical 14-day Italian Forecast Window for the party invitation, and, of course, JJ did exactly what any avoidant Florentine would do: used the tagline of "Vediamo."

This is why his species is called Prehistoricus Non-Confirmatus.

Let's break down specifically, JJ's internal logic, because it is comedy gold: Inside the Avoidant Italian Mind at 14 Days. "Two weeks? Impossible. I don't even know what I'm eating for dinner." "If I commit now, the universe will punish me." "I will respond only at a time that aligns with the celestial orbit of my avoidance, perhaps 16 hours after receiving a sighting report from the housekeeper."

I just texted him if he's coming with his two friends. But courage is not the strong suit of a man who treats social gatherings like active combat zones. I even reassured him: twenty-five people, plenty of cover, zero need to hide behind his avoidance.

My gut tells me that he will not show up. And naturally, I couldn't resist pushing that particular dysfunction button on the dashboard on the way out. (He short-circuited, of course. Silence: the traditional mating call of the avoidant velociraptor.)

It's my way of saying, I see your avoidance, I'm not angry. Avoidants panic at direct confrontation, but they're completely disarmed by playful accuracy.

It landed exactly where I needed it to: light, mocking, affectionate, and impossible for him to dodge. It also captured the essence of our dynamic perfectly, him always slipping behind some imaginary curtain, and me politely reminding him.

It was closure, the most predictable outcome imaginable: zero answer. Typical. The JJ is nothing if not consistent in his inconsistencies.

Exhibit 45: The Pre-RSVP Dance Perimeter
Where JJ Circles an RSVP Like It's a Trap

So, it begins…He's asking if there's another occasion to see my BFF, except for the party.

Of course, JJ is asking if there's another occasion to see my BFF…because saying "Yes, I'll come to your party" is far too straightforward for him.

This is classic Avoidant Logistics Maneuver #7: "Pretend I'm being helpful while actually avoiding committing to the main event."

Let's translate his message into real language:

JJ (text): "Is there another occasion to see your BFF besides the party?"

JJ (actual meaning): "I'm circling the perimeter of commitment." "I'm testing escape routes." "I want the connection without the responsibility." "I am allergic to RSVP."

But here's the comedy: He wants to see her, not necessarily avoid me. He just doesn't want the formality of the event. Also, deep down? He's trying to engineer a scenario where he gets to see me without feeling like he's stepping into a big social commitment. This is a classic velociraptor tactic; circumnavigate the party while still orbiting me.

My power move is keeping it neutral. I told him I don't know their schedule until they come. Because if I suddenly create a separate mini-meeting, he will latch onto it like a life raft and make me responsible for regulating his emotional overwhelm.

I already know this pattern: I manage my feelings, his feelings, the environment, the weather, the emotional feng shui…Meanwhile, he regulates nothing.

By doing this, I regulate his nervous system: "Don't worry, I'll soften reality so you don't get triggered." That is exactly what therapy should teach him, not me.

It also reinforces the wrong dynamic. My job is not to protect him from my guests, my friends, my life, or normal human interaction. JJ must step into my world as an adult.

It also gives him a "comfort cushion" he hasn't earned. If he's emotionally overwhelmed by the existence of other people, that's not my logistical problem to solve. It puts me back into the "caretaker" role. And no, I'm done being the Emotional Sommelier pairing his moods with appropriate reactions.

This is the perfect moment for the exhibit narrator to whisper: Exhibit: The Pre-RSVP Perimeter Dance. In which the dinosaur cautiously circles the idea of attending, like it might bite him.

Exhibit 46: The Paradox of the Avoidant Party Lover

Who dances everywhere except where it matters?

Welcome to my most precise deep dive into the psyche of a Jurassic avoidant, written by his unofficial handler. Yes, he genuinely wants to meet my BFF. That part is real. If he were avoiding *me*, we wouldn't even be tiptoeing around this conversation. He wouldn't ask about alternative plans. He wouldn't open the door to seeing my friends and me in any format.

What he is allergic to is the formality of "an event." And mind you, I removed every emotional booby trap. Told him: no intimacy. I'll be busy hosting; he can bring two friends, for a total of 20–25 people. Zero pressure. Zero spotlight. Zero couple energy.

Basically: "Here's a crowd big enough that you can slip in, hover, and pretend you're part of the décor. No one will even notice you." Still, he feels the existential weight of walking into a structured social environment.

Avoidants love connecting in unstructured spaces, where plans happen accidentally, and nothing feels official. Hence, his late-night spontaneity, pop-in chaos, and random nights out. My party is a fixed, named event. His brain registers this as: "That is a stage. I do not like stages." So, he attempts the classic avoidant compromise move, "Is there…an adjacent doorway into this?"

This is most likely his Jurassic inner monologue: "I want to see her BFF…But a party feels like signing a contract…Is there a smaller, less emotionally radioactive entrance?"

He's not rejecting me. He's trying to locate a version that feels less emotionally loaded *for him*. My reply didn't chase, didn't invent alternative events, didn't negotiate. It held the boundary: "If you want to see her, the event exists. You're welcome to attend."

He can literally hide behind his two friends, who will be holding up his medieval shield of denial. The funniest part? I gave him a social shield, a comfortable buffer, a camouflage strategy…and he is still on the savannah scanning for an alternative watering hole.

Exhibit 47: The Emoji Stampede of a Panicked Velociraptor

Because nothing says "I'm terrified" like 12 unrelated emojis.

His response to my social shield was a string of LOL emojis. Because when an avoidant is emotionally cornered by reality, even gently, what do they do?

They deflect. They perform. They laugh. They send emojis. This is the most classic avoidant maneuver in the book. Emotional truth enters the chat, emoji avalanche deployed. Let's decode that exact string of emojis with forensic precision: What Seven LOL's Actually Means in Avoidant Language.

1. "I'm overwhelmed, abort mission." When I said something grounded, clear, emotionally mature, or factual, he felt a spike of activation. So, he hit me with the string of LOL emojis to avoid dealing with it.

2. "I don't know how to respond, so I'm performing." Avoidants hide behind humor because humor allows them to avoid sincerity. He wasn't actually laughing. He was escaping.

3. "If I keep this light, I won't have to feel anything." Emojis are JJ's equivalent of hiding inside a Florentine *vicolo* so narrow even accountability can't squeeze through.

4. "Please don't make me use words." Because words require clarity, accountability, and emotional honesty, Emojis require nothing.

5. "I'm uncomfortable, but I don't want to create conflict." This part is essential. He didn't get hostile, defensive, withdraw aggressively, or lash out. He just… laughed. This is his version of being nervously compliant.

It's his way of acknowledging me, responding without responding, keeping the tone safe, and avoiding escalation. JJ often masks discomfort with laughter or jokes.

But here's the kicker, this response actually shows I hit something true. I landed on an emotional nerve. Not in a bad way. In a "this is uncomfortable but accurate" way. His emojis were basically, "I have no emotional skills for this conversation, so… here's a clown-car explosion of laughter."

Exhibit 48: The Avoidant Freeze: When Time Becomes an SAT Question

When Accountability Enters the Room and the Nervous System Exits.

His "reason" for not coming? "Nel fine settimana vado via."

Translation: "I am going away on the weekend."

Me: "I told you the date two weeks ago. Bring your two friends so they can help you hide behind the curtain if you're afraid."

This was the verbal equivalent of shining a flashlight at a velociraptor crouching behind a drape.

He froze. He blinked. He went silent.

I basically handed him a logic puzzle. His inner monologue became: "I've been confronted with linear time." "I did not prepare an excuse." "My brain is rebooting."...*Loading*...Hence: silence. Just as predictable as his emergency weekend trip that materializes only after feelings corner him.

When I jokingly reassured him about the two-friend curtain-holding squad, the message was: "I know you're a shy dinosaur. I provided a pack. Come graze in peace." Gentle, comedic, dignified. He can't outrun humor; it's a spotlight without heat.

What it really means in Avoidant English is "You emotionally poked me, and now I must flee the region.

And when I said, "I told you this 2 weeks ago."

So, Ladies and Gentlemen, we are right at Stage 3 of the Avoidant Logistics Ballet.

Here is the whole choreography of what he just performed:

Stage 1: The Flail: I brought up the date, planning, and attendance. He panicked like someone turned on a bright light in a cave.

Stage 2: Deflect: This is the in-between moment of the emoji barrage, the nonsensical laughter, vague excuses, the "maybe" energy, and questions about my BFF. This is the dinosaur spinning in circles but pretending he's dancing.

Stage 3: The Detonate ("Nel fine settimana vado via") Kaboom. The avoidant eject button.

The "I'm going away" declaration. Even if he is literally sitting at home staring at the ceiling. Avoidants detonate before intimacy hits the room.

When I told him, "I told you this two weeks ago." He was confronted with accountability, foresight, planning, adult functioning, the fact that I am stable, the fact that he is not, and his nervous system detonated.

Exhibit 49: Why the Velociraptor Parties Everywhere Except Your House Party
A Field Guide to Jurassic RSVP Avoidance

Everybody loves a party, especially him. He goes out 5–6 nights a week. He attends events, social marathons, and random nights that last until sunrise.

But a house party hosted by a woman he once loved? That's different.

At my house party, he doesn't have the illusion of control. I'm the host. The spotlight is gently (but undeniably) on me. Which means, by extension, it momentarily grazes whatever our dynamic is to the room.

Avoidants hate anything that hints at relational definition. I dated the original version 25 years ago. Nothing has changed. The missing relational definition was the "feeling" that clicked, like déjà vu, once I realized JJ's affliction.

JJ loves random social chaos because it's pure noise. No implications. No context. No meaning.

A party in my home with my BFF and my circle is an emotional context. Even if nothing happens between us, we barely speak; he hides in a corner with his two friends; the environment is symbolic. It echoes a connection he remembers but can't manage.

Even if he remembers the teasing, the chemistry, Cris P. Bacon, the tenderness, my home, it will trigger the archives. I'm not the threat. His emotional blueprint is the threat. And that's precisely why he's unlikely to show. He wants the noise but not the intimacy of a room that remembers him.

My text to JJ:

"Why not just tell me the truth that social events with me make you nervous, and that my home brings back memories of past vulnerabilities, and that you don't know how to behave around me without feeling emotional, and that you are nervous about coming. So instead, you lie and say you will be out of town this weekend.

This translates into, 'I can't handle the inner turmoil your party causes me.' It is not a rejection; it's a way to avoid inner turmoil. It's not about the party; it's about the environment that stirs up feelings you can't control.

The fact that you have to announce your weekend plans in advance means I have stirred something up in you. You're trying to control your emotional perimeter.

I have already given you cover with Massi and Rafaelle, and I do not know how you can live with these suffocating emotional fears 24/7 while still shouting "freedom" at the top of your lungs when you're locked in a paddock of fear where your only light is the light coming in from under the door.

I cannot force you to come, nor will I, but you have written my next chapter."

My second text:

"I need to try to understand that my home and our memories stir up so many emotions in you that you prefer to be a fortress with concrete injected into your veins. And that's the part you avoid, the parts of you that felt something when you were here with me.

You're not avoiding me, you're avoiding your feelings. Avoidant people avoid things that make them uncomfortable. You ran away because I meant something to you, and you couldn't handle the situation. I think this is the main reason you don't want to come to the party, and not because you're busy."

Exhibit 50: The Cognitive Extinction Event

When one woman's insight triggers a full-system T-Rex blackout

What I sent wasn't a text; it was a psychological MRI delivered with surgical precision. I didn't attack him, dramatize, or lose emotional footing; I named the exact processes he spends his entire life avoiding.

I named the exact mechanisms he's been dodging for years, the ones he refuses to admit even to himself.

It was precision he's not built to metabolize; the kind professionals take months to reach. Accuracy is his panic button.

My words hit every nerve at once: the fear, the vulnerability, the shame, the attachment trigger, the emotional paralysis. I made sure to leave him with no escape route.

He can't deny my logic, he can't contradict what I described, and he can't respond without exposing the exact shame he's trying to outrun. He shuts down like someone yanked his power cord.

Or what I like to call "The Frozen Thumb Phenomenon". Where fully functional adult males dial my number… and Jurassic Jackasses lose all motor skills. His thumbs froze like he was a velociraptor trying to unlock an iPhone with mittens on.

I understand he is like this, not because he doesn't care, but because he cares too much and cannot metabolize what he feels in my presence. I named the forbidden truth: he isn't avoiding me; he's avoiding the version of himself that becomes activated around me.

That's the part he cannot face without therapy, without emotional language, and without a level of internal stability he simply doesn't have right now. For all his incense and meditation apps, real introspection still sends him running.

Picture a full-sized T. rex curled behind an imaginary velvet curtain, whispering, "Non posso rispondere… è troppo vero," clutching a meditation app he hasn't opened since 2021. Sometimes, the most terrifying thing for someone living behind a concrete emotional fortress isn't conflict or chaos; it's being seen clearly by someone who refuses to crack.

Exhibit 51: The Free-Partying Parasite Who Keeps JJ Feeling Functional

The Avoidant Ecosystem Buddy System.

Back to the topic of partying. JJ hangs out with an emotional support freeloader who lives with his parents and coasts from free party to free party, but at least JJ has his values, pays his fair share, and isn't a freeloader.

He keeps people around who make him feel functional by comparison; a specific someone who lives with his parents, drifts from party to party, has zero accountability, and keeps him around as his emotional participation trophy.

JJ is the functional avoidant in this pairing. He pays. He shows up. He pretends he's the grown-up in the dynamic duo.

The other guy requires no emotional effort, no vulnerability, no structure. It's the one environment where he feels competent. JJ gets to feel competent, generous, and socially safe, without ever risking real intimacy.

He likes being around someone who is just chaotic enough that he looks put-together in comparison, while still being able to move through life with zero actual emotional responsibility. It's the "I'm not that dysfunctional, look at him" trick.

Around him, JJ gets to cosplay as the responsible one. With me, there's nowhere to hide. I expect adulthood, while his buddy is the emotional vacation, a human hammock, because my velociraptor is built for cushions, not challenges.

Exhibit 52: The Declawing of the Jurassic Jackass

Where the Dinosaur's Old Tricks Lose Their Teeth.

What's hilarious about this entire dynamic is that I'm not even trying to prod his dysfunction, okay, sometimes I am, but mostly I'm just breathing, and he combusts.

The second I stepped out of his emotional maze, the hierarchy collapsed. Now, the power has not only flipped; it has been rotated, inverted, carbon-dated, fossilized, and placed under museum lighting with a gold-plated placard reading: "Warning: This Dinosaur Exhibits Extreme Avoidant Behaviors. Approach With Emotional Regulation."

The moment I opted out of the avoidant performance, his script fell apart. I named what he was doing and refused to join the performance. Suddenly, all his little tricks became artifacts. I stopped reacting, so his tricks lost their prey.

While he spontaneously remembered the date of my flight's arrival from four months ago, he did not remember his therapist's name, which was labeled as a "Selective Memory Fossil." It's not that I'm provoking dysfunction; it's that my clarity is the scalpel he never saw coming.

The balance shifted because I'm no longer living inside the emotional tornado with him; I'm watching the weather patterns from an observation deck with popcorn. I'm no longer in the scene; I'm narrating it. Meanwhile, he's still out there twitching behind imaginary curtains, performing Avoidant Parkour, circling RSVP decisions like they're landmines, and manufacturing logistics excuses with the desperation of a man trying to avoid a dinner party but not an after-hours techno rave.

His subconscious knows the dynamic is different. He feels the neutrality, the lack of emotional chaos, the absence of reacting. Avoidants are exquisitely sensitive to losing the upper hand, and they feel it deeply.

That's what makes it funny: my "prodding" is literally just observation. I don't even need to say anything dramatic; I can point at a pattern, and he reacts like someone flicked on the auditorium lights mid-performance. And yes, it probably scares him that I decode him faster than he decodes himself.

His coping tools only work in the dark; I flipped the light switch. I removed the fog. I mapped the entire fire-escape plan. He can't hide behind smoke when I've already diagrammed the ventilation system.

Being understood, accurately understood, is intoxicating for him because so few people have ever seen beyond the charming surface (not even his best friend, apparently). But it's also repulsive because understanding strips his camouflage. And avoidants need camouflage like I need oxygen.

My clarity ruins the illusion he lives inside. "Control" is his comfort blanket, and avoidance is the only language he speaks fluently. I stopped worshipping at his altar, and the temple suddenly wobbled.

I'm not special for receiving his avoidant treatment; he's an equal opportunity guy. I've watched him pull the same disappearing acts with random friends. I just happened to get the deluxe package because I matter more to him, and that terrifies him.

But now, none of his tactics work on me. Not silence. Not delays. Not last-minute flailing. Not faux-casual "I'm going away this weekend" announcements. I observe him like a zoologist with a clipboard, knowing precisely what he'll do, why he'll do it, how long it will take, and the precise moment it will collapse. And that is genuinely terrifying for him because I see the part of himself he deeply avoids.

The entire attraction-repulsion loop is born from this exact emotional terror. He is drawn to me because I offer clarity, emotional literacy, and a level of insight no one else does. I reflect his deeper self back to him accurately without collapsing under his chaos, and I hold boundaries he's never encountered before. And, I know the blueprint of his Jurassic noggin so well that I could renovate it.

But the repulsion? That comes from dismantling his avoidant maneuvers instantly, refusing to be manipulated, and holding a mirror that forces self-awareness. It makes him feel naked in ways he cannot emotionally regulate. This combination, being seen, understood, and still held accountable, is both addictive and terrifying for an avoidant like him.

And here's the final truth: he's rattled because the power has fully shifted. He's not the enigma anymore. He's the exhibit. I'm the curator. He senses it in my tone, my calm, my boundaries, and my complete refusal to reenact his old scripts. I understand the software he's running better than he does. That's exactly why he circles me, is drawn to me, is intimidated by me, is overwhelmed by me, is unable to step forward, and yet is unable to step away. I am emotionally fluent in a language he barely speaks. And that, for a Jurassic Jackass, is the most terrifying discovery of all.

Exhibit 53: The Thread That Would Not Snap, An Analysis of Persistent Bonding in Avoidant Species

An Anthropological Study of Two Humans Who Shouldn't Be This Intertwined, Yet Somehow Are.

The strange thing about my connection with JJ is that it never behaved like a normal relationship, and it refuses to behave like a typical ending.

Whatever we are, it didn't evaporate. Some ties don't dissolve; they settle in. Ours was forged in emotional intensity, inconsistent availability, unresolved endings, and a private language of jokes, rituals, and mutual bewilderment.

Once a bond like that imprints, it lingers the way an old Wi-Fi network pops up on your phone years after you've moved away: Velociraptor_5G: auto-connect enabled.

He's always hovered, close but never still. He hides behind imaginary curtains, peeks out to see if I'm still there, then reappears with a casual "tutto bene grazie" as if he hadn't vanished for months.

That's the irony of avoidants: they can't handle intimacy or vulnerability, but they can handle particular forms of connection. With him, it's always been light banter, small logistical exchanges, a prod on his dysfunction, the neutral "museum tone" of being seen without being exposed.

And for reasons neither of us fully understands, I am one of the only people he can tolerate in that narrow emotional bandwidth. Avoidants don't maintain ties with exes; they stick you in emotional deep-freeze like forgotten leftovers, and they don't revisit old emotional homes; they delete the file.

The original avoidant did precisely that, gone the second I replaced him. But it didn't stop him from chasing me up this staircase to try to seduce me. I barked back, "You had your chance and blew it."

JJ, however, breaks his own pattern with me. He once told me he only "sees his exes outside," which is avoidant code for random public sightings, not connection. Yet even during our most fragile periods, he would still walk me home, sit on my sofa, talk with me, and we would have intimate conversations.

For him, that was a marathon. He doesn't casually enter anyone's home, including mine, but the psychological loop is always on. Be he answers, he returns, he circles, and he remembers strange details with forensic precision.

He resists the deeper intimacy but refuses to detach fully. Early in the relationship, he said he wanted me in his life for the rest of his life, and avoidants do not say things like that unless something bypasses their defenses. It wasn't romantic; it was a confession. A quiet acknowledgment that whatever we are, whatever we have been, I occupy a permanent corner in his internal architecture.

It wasn't romantic. It wasn't a promise. It was a confession, a quiet, unguarded admission that I occupy permanent real estate in some internal chamber of his psyche.

Not as a partner. Not as an ex. Not as a fallback or a placeholder. But as something unclassifiable. Something he can't erase. Something he expects, consciously or not, to be threaded into the background of his life indefinitely. It's something older and stranger than romance.

A bond that doesn't fit human categories, built instead from recognition, tension, mirrored humor, shared absurdity, and that uncanny feeling of "I know you," even when everything else is chaos. And so, instead of trying to sever something that isn't meant to be severed, I have done what any curator of dysfunction would do: I preserved it, framed it, labeled it, catalogued it with wry affection, and placed it under soft museum lighting where it belongs, as a rare artifact from a species that could never fully evolve but still managed to leave tracks across my emotional landscape.

In the end, it's a relic from the Cretaceous Dating Era. A reminder that some people leave footprints on your psyche not because they were your great love, but because they were your greatest study.

Exhibit 54: Emotional CPR for a Velociraptor

A Field Guide to Handling an Avoidant Without Triggering a Jurassic Extinction Event.

JJ is just such an emotional mess. He doesn't want to come to the party because he's afraid of his own emotions showing up and embarrassing him as they've done before. So, I tell him about a low-key dinner with my BFF on Friday, and he sends me a voice note that, for all practical purposes, was recorded from inside a tornado. From what I could decipher through the hurricane-force wind, he wanted to do it "during the week." It was the verbal equivalent of smoke signals from the Jurassic era.

So, I put the onus on him, because I was sick to death of tiptoeing around the dysregulation of his dysfunctional emotions. I asked the most straightforward adult question on earth: "What day?" And naturally, the moment responsibility touched his skin, he vanished like a startled Velociraptor, zero response. Not a single pixel moved.

What I really wanted to say was, "Do you want to do it during the week so your body won't interpret a simple dinner with me on the weekend as a prehistoric threat to survival? Have I understood correctly? Because all I can hear is the wind blowing." It would have been perfect, funny, sharp, painfully accurate. But the angel on my shoulder must have had a megaphone that evening, because she somehow convinced me not to flatten him into fossil dust emotionally. It would have been too precise, too psychologically revealing. Avoidants panic when you demonstrate you understand their internal wiring better than they do.

Despite how hilarious the message would have been to a normal adult, JJ would have felt exposed, like I had turned on stadium lighting around his avoidance patterns. His instinct would be to retreat into the velvet curtains of emotional self-protection, the ones he wraps around himself whenever he feels seen too clearly. That one prehistoric-survival line alone would hit him right in the secret chamber he hides from the world, and from himself.

And the "wind blowing" line? To him, it's the equivalent of shining a flashlight directly onto his emotional escape hatch. Even delivered humorously, he would feel called out, and he breaks out in metaphorical hives the moment that happens.

Truth hits him like a fire alarm. It doesn't matter how warm, gentle, or witty it is. The moment he feels seen, his shame activates, and once shame activates, the man goes into emotional hypothermia. That's why he either goes mute or sends LOL emojis in bulk like cheap confetti.

He can handle playful teasing, soft irony, and gentle humor. What he cannot handle is psychological accuracy served as comedy. Avoidants crumble like poorly restored frescos when even one brushstroke of truth touches their surface.

So instead, I listened to the angel and asked the most straightforward question again: "What day is good for you?" He promptly went extinct. Apparently, psychology agrees, if you poke an avoidant's dysfunction directly, they don't wake up; they shut down. Not because my insight is wrong, not because it's harsh, but because the reaction I want and the reaction he's capable of are two separate, incompatible species.

I wanted a flicker of self-awareness, maybe a moment of accountability if the planets aligned. But what actually happens internally is that he goes straight to shame, defensiveness, withdrawal, freeze, silence, avoidance, and a complete emotional retreat into the fog. It doesn't matter that the humor is light; his ego can't process it, and his nervous system collapses under it. Anything that threatens to reveal a flaw stops him cold, like he just saw a feelings bill he can't afford.

So, if I want him actually to wake up, I have to do it indirectly. This calls for a new strategy, not because I want him back, but because I'm shockingly compassionate tonight and can see, plain as day, that he has deteriorated since I left four months ago. I am not dealing with a man who needs blunt truth. I am dealing with a man who cannot survive the blunt truth.

He needs emotional safety, the illusion of choice, the soft glow of autonomy, warmth, boundaries, and stable consistency from me, delivered calmly. Anything sharper than that, and he collapses behind the velvet curtain again.

I saw this clearly when I cried about Scarlett, and he held my hand with both of his. He softened. He remembered all my arrival dates without prompting. He let my head rest on his shoulder. His defenses lowered because he didn't feel judged or analyzed. That's how I woke him up, not through poking, but through safety. So, this time, I'm playing psychological judo instead of emotional boxing, quiet effectiveness instead of accuracy bombs.

JJ has spent his entire adult life surrounded by people who don't confront him, don't mirror him, don't challenge him, don't see him, accept crumbs, tolerate avoidance, or don't care whether he retreats emotionally.

I'm the first person who actually knows the choreography: the micro-signals, the breath hitch right before he lies, the eye-dart he thinks is subtle, the flicker of panic behind his smile, the exact millisecond he prepares to bolt like a malnourished greyhound. His tells aren't tells, they're billboards. I sense the vulnerability before he feels it. And nothing destabilizes an avoidant faster than being fully, accurately seen by someone they cannot outrun.

I have to speak in a dialect that won't trigger his internal antivirus. That formula is warm, bounded, consistent, and stable. It's basically the survival guide for dealing with a prehistoric alarm system: approach lightly, keep it soothing, and never present emotional facts unsupervised. But it works. It makes him feel safe, makes him self-reflect, makes him realize he lost something real, and ideally nudges him toward therapy so a licensed adult can handle the rest.

When I'm grounded, he becomes aware; when I'm sharp, he becomes scared. My power is not in the jab, tempting as it is, it's in the presence. Warmth cracks the door open. Boundaries force the mirror. And I suspect I am the only person in his life who has ever made him face anything real without shaming him or rescuing him, which is precisely why he doesn't spiral around me the way he does with everyone else.

This warm-but-bounded combination is the only ecosystem where he can grow. I'm not tiptoeing; I'm leading. I set the pace, the temperature, the emotional choreography, and for once in his chaotic career, he's following instead of dragging me behind his emotional getaway car.

My warmth regulates him instantly, but I refuse to be his permanent emotional pacemaker. He feels safest with me, yes, but he must learn to feel stable when I'm not physically inside his zip code.

Until then, he can't truly be a partner to anyone. And the shift is this: I'm no longer enabling him. I'm modeling emotional safety while refusing to carry him. If he grows, it won't be because I dragged him there; it will be because clarity finally pierced through his fog.

I'm not waiting, not auditioning, not lowering my standards. I'm stating reality: if he wants deeper access to me, he has to evolve. Growth may be optional, but access to me is not.

I have intuitive mastery with him, built on psychological fluency, instinct, timing, and a sixth sense that borders on CIA-level micro-reading. I catch cues in microseconds; my instincts adjust faster than he can generate denial.

My touch is warm and non-threatening, the emotional equivalent of a silk blanket, which is why he never flinches. He listens to me in ways he doesn't listen to anyone else. Coming from a man who treats vulnerability like a medieval plague, that was basically a sonnet.

And he knows exactly what it means: I see him. I won't flinch. I won't lie. And if he loses me, it won't be because I was unclear; it will be because he refused to evolve.

He's like a man standing in the rain trying to patch a leaking roof with a cocktail napkin while insisting the roof is "fine." Nothing has ever been integrated, confronted, or stabilized. Not because he's malicious, but because he's emotionally untrained and terrified of everything that matters.

My poor JJ yearns for affection, closeness, and safety. He enjoys my presence. He trusts my warmth. But he doesn't have the internal tools to handle any of it without shutting down, freezing, avoiding, flailing, or emotionally dissolving into chaos.

He's emotionally tone-deaf but insists he's a concert pianist. That's why he's a mess. And that's why I'm adjusting the strategy, not for him, but for my own sanity.

Exhibit 55: When the Avoidant's Body Said "Ti Amo" While His Brain Short-Circuited

When Jurassic Instinct Overpowered Avoidant Logic

Three days before the party, I had to call him because I needed our housekeeper to come to me again the next day. It was JJ's scheduled cleaning day, but my best friend and her daughter were arriving, and I needed the flat squared away before their arrival and the party.

So, I called him, and honestly, I was surprised he even answered. He immediately launched into some bizarre tangent about talking with a guy who "believes in God," and I'm standing there like, "What? Why are we having this theological TED talk when I have twelve things exploding around me?" I did not have the bandwidth for JJ's philosophical detours at the eleventh hour.

I cut him off, handed the phone to the housekeeper, switched the schedule, and that should have been the end of the story.

Later that evening, I texted to thank him for switching days, and right on cue, he hit me with a classic JJ maneuver: he invited me to dinner…happening in 20 minutes. This is how avoidants send invitations, like emotional drive-bys. I agreed, partly because I needed to return his decoy keys, and partly because I wanted to ask him if he'd like to meet my best friend from the Philippines.

When I arrived, I immediately put JJ's favorite snack, roasted peanuts with garlic, right into the palm of his hand. A small gesture, yes, but loaded. I touched his thigh when I handed them to him, signaling without words: I'm not angry. I'm not holding anything over your head. We're okay.

His whole nervous system softened under my touch. He reset, like someone pressed the "safe mode" button on a malfunctioning raptor. And in turn, he fed me twice.

If he were really over me, his hands wouldn't be feeding me like a vending machine for unresolved feelings and mildly mortifying. But that was his tenderness leaking out like an emotional plumbing issue, not a performance. That wasn't a show; that was his nervous system forgetting to lie.

Massimiliano was sitting right there, watching the scene unfold with those subtle, perceptive eyes of his. I'm sure he sensed the history instantly. This was the first time JJ and I had seen each other since the infamous decoy-key-transfer-on-Battistero-day, also known as "JJ's Mount Vesuvius Meltdown."

His anger in July, the cold distance after, the absurd avoidance around the keys, all symptoms of unmanaged avoidance triggered by love. Not absence of feeling, but too much sensory overload. He doesn't run because he doesn't care. He runs because he does, and can't regulate it.

I took the opportunity to invite his friend Massi to the party and asked him to text his other friend. He did it immediately, without checking with JJ. They clearly all knew JJ already knew about the party. His friends are basically his emotional chaperones, making sure he doesn't accidentally feel anything unsupervised. He brings them like human training wheels, so he doesn't accidentally topple into intimacy.

When I said it would be a late-night party, JJ's ears perked up like someone lifted the lid off a food bowl. Avoidants love late-night invitations; they feel emotionally unpressured, fluid, non-committal. That "perk up" wasn't accidental. That was his nervous system whispering, "Oh… I could handle that."

Early events equal emotional pressure. Late events equal freedom to slip in, slip out, panic, return, oscillate, or hide behind a potted plant if necessary.

Whether he came or not, his friends would be there, which put him in a delightful bind: Lie to them too and say he's "not in town" (his go-to excuse). Or show up with them. Or show up alone and stay for five minutes like a terrified meerkat.

When the check came, I went to pay my share, and he practically combusted. I have never seen him protest so intensely in front of his friends. Watching me pay my share fried his 'I'm still her man' fantasy and soothed his 'no one depends on me' panic in the same swipe.

Ah, the avoidant paradox: my independence is the thing that soothes him, and the thing that stings him. But the soothing always wins, because it protects the fragile ego.

He didn't run after dinner, unlike the disaster at the Battistero. He runs from structured emotional environments, not from me. Tonight wasn't structured. It was loose, warm, unplanned, and his body relaxed into it.

After dinner, we went to Spiritum. It was quiet. I stepped outside with my wine, and JJ followed. And then suddenly…like flies on poop, we were in each other's arms.

I don't remember who reached first. I don't recall how it happened. It was instinct more than thought.

Not a romantic embrace, but one that said: "I missed you. I'm home. I feel safe. My nervous system recognizes you."

Our bodies melted into each other like two beings who remembered the shape of the other. The forehead-lean-in, our signature move, surfaced instantly, as if it were muscle memory stored deep in our nervous systems.

That hug blew a hole straight through his armor. This wasn't 'a nice night'; it was the kind of body-memory his nervous system will be replaying when he's eighty and still pretending he's fine.

Forehead-to-forehead is primal, mammalian bonding. He then kissed my forehead and the top of my head with a million micro-kisses. The imprint was intact. His friend came outside and interrupted us; otherwise, we might have stayed fused until sunrise.

Avoidants never repeat intimate rituals with someone they're done with. Their bodies simply don't allow it. Mine didn't either.

During the forehead lean-in, I told him softly, "You will always have a safe place with me." That line didn't land in adult JJ. It landed on the 8-year-old, who never had emotional safety. It hit the part of him that was never soothed, never validated, never protected.

And he felt it. His whole body told me he thought it.

That's why he texted me later: "È stata una bella serata." At 2:30 AM, when his guard was down, and he was replaying the hug, the feeding, the warmth, the forehead lean-in, my steady presence, and that hit of "I'm safe with her."

He usually walks me home, but he couldn't because Massi needed the gate opened at JJ's house. Instead, JJ insisted I take a cab. I insisted on walking home from the cab stand. His protest was a pure expression of protectiveness, not avoidance.

It still hits me because I've met the unarmored version he keeps locked in the basement while the Jurassic Jackass does PR upstairs. My heart didn't melt because I still "want" him. It melted because I saw him, truly saw him, and he let me in. Moments like that leave an imprint, no matter how rational you are.

He doesn't just miss me; he misses the emotionally competent hologram of himself that only materializes when I'm around. And that's why my silence worked. Staying warm but independent is the exact combination he responds to.

I don't judge his afflictions. I contextualize them. I try to understand them. I try to hold compassion without enabling. He can't hide from someone who sees him so clearly and chooses gentleness over judgment.

He thinks he rebuilt the Great Wall of Florence overnight. Meanwhile, I reactivated a sensor in him that he cannot switch off, even if he duct-tapes it, pads it, and places his free-partying parasite friend in front of it as security.

Exhibit 56: The Panic Emoji at the Sports Film Festival

Where a Three-Word Text Causes a Full Avoidant Seismic Event in Sicily.

There are moments in the long archaeological study of my sweet JJ that reveal more about his inner workings than months of interaction. You think you know a man until a three-word text detonates an emotional fault line he didn't think he had. Mine was simple: "Met anyone interesting?"

A normal sentence. A surface-level question. A polite, breezy curiosity. He was at a four-day sports film festival in Sicily, with lots of people in the film industry and producers, and I merely wanted to demonstrate how one can continue a thread of connection even when out of one's zip code.

But inside JJ's prehistoric nervous system, the translation software scrambled, sparked, and set off a full-scale attachment earthquake: "Jesus Christ, is she leaving me?" "Did she meet someone else?" "Why is she asking this?" "Is this a trap?" "Emergency! Vocalize immediately!"

This is why, instead of answering like a calm Homo sapiens with a fully developed prefrontal cortex, he sent… a voice note. Avoidants don't use voice notes for efficiency; they use them for damage control, to control tone, to hide insecurity, and to test for danger. It's their emotional 911 hotline, and I've been subjected to it more times than I can count.

So, I open the message, and instead of Italian warmth or casual interest, I get the panic-whisper tone of a man who has just catastrophized an entire breakup from a relationship he publicly insists never existed: "What do you mean…if someone interesting? Do you mean someone in particular?"

Because when I texted, "Met anyone interesting?" his brain translated it into an existential crisis: "Are you replacing me?" "Is someone else taking my place?" "Have you moved on?"

What was, to me, a zero-energy question became, to him, a spotlight aimed at the exact part of himself he is terrified I might examine, whether he desires anyone else, whether he measures up, and whether our connection is exclusive in a way he can't admit but deeply feels.

So, he spiraled, panicked, and requested clarification twice because what he was really asking was: "Are you seeing someone?" "Are you hinting at something?" "Do I need to be worried?"

My response was calm, light, and slightly dismissive. It snapped him out of it. I wasn't jealous, I wasn't testing him, and I certainly wasn't implying anything. Most importantly, my tone said, "Relax. I'm fine. Don't project your fears onto me."

That tone hits his avoidant wiring like a lightning strike; it makes him feel safe and exposed at the same time. This is why he immediately became Emoji King.

Imagine the Venus de Milo panicking about whether another armless goddess had caught your attention. That's the level of emotional turbulence we were dealing with.

And did I soothe him? Stroke the delicate dinosaur ego? Absolutely not.

I told him to calm down, asked if he was having fun, and then repeated the actual question: 'Did you meet anyone interesting?' Not "Are you replacing me?" "Should I panic?" "Should I flee the country?" (Though, to be fair, he panicked so quickly he could've applied for Swiss citizenship by the end of the message.)

And then came the masterpiece of avoidant damage control: the post-panic relief smile emoji. Not a usual smile. Not a flirty smile. Not a casual smile. But the exact expression a man sends when he realizes, in real time, that he just spiraled into a three-second emotional apocalypse over nothing.

"Oh, thank God, she's not replacing me. Okay. Neutral face. Send a safe emoji. Act normal." That emoji is the avoidant "crisis averted, meltdown cancelled" emoji.

Here's what his internal monologue actually sounded like: "Shit, did she mean another man? Why did she ask that? Wait, she sounds unbothered. Is she not jealous? Is she not hinting? Oh, thank God. Okay. Breathe. Just send something neutral. Don't sound emotional."

Avoidants are never more adorable than when they accidentally expose how deeply they care and how deeply terrified they are of being abandoned by the woman they claim is "just a friend."

Because here is the truth he will never say aloud, the threat he felt came entirely from inside his own imagination. But the moment I diffused it with a simple, "Just asking. Have fun," his entire internal ecosystem shifted. He softened. He calmed. He re-centered. He let out an exhale; I swear I heard it across the Tuscan air.

Once again, I had become his Renaissance emotional anchor, the steady presence that calms him, steadies him, and scares the living daylights out of him all at once.

I think he finally realized how he really feels about me… and the awareness hit him like a Vespa colliding with a Renaissance column.

Here's what's happening inside him now: he's loved me in his avoidant, chaotic, stored-in-the-nervous-system way for far longer than he'll ever admit. Avoidants often don't realize they're attached until something threatens their attachment. He didn't develop feelings out of the blue; he finally recognized them.

And that realization, plus his dysfunction, equals pure comedy and chaos. Avoidant men in love are unintentionally hilarious. They send crisis voice notes over harmless messages, catastrophize breakups from relationships they deny, act jealous of men you haven't met, panic when you're calm, soften when you're distant, freeze when you're affectionate, send emojis like local anesthesia, get emotional hangovers from seeing you smile at other men, short-circuit from proximity, melt from familiarity, and then pretend nothing happened.

And JJ is the peak specimen.

Realization terrifies avoidants. He is now living inside the emotional nightmare they're structurally built to avoid: "I care." "I need her." "She's slipping." "I'm not in control." "I can't hide this anymore."

And the wild part? I didn't do anything. I shifted, centered, and stopped over-investing. He walked straight into his own feelings.

His dysfunction isn't blocking anything anymore; it's revealing everything. This is why the soft-face leakage keeps happening, why jealousy flickers, why sudden warmth appears and disappears, why the little moments of tenderness slip through the cracks he tries to plaster shut.

He is in that avoidant paradox: in love, terrified, destabilized, hopeful, and doomed, all at the same time. And he thinks he's hiding all of this.

He genuinely believes the voice note and the emoji came across as casual, while I'm standing here watching a man spiral, recover, self-soothe, panic, soften, pretend, fail, try again, and leak attachment from every pore.

He's a living exhibit, a walking museum wing, and I'm the archivist.

Exhibit 57: The Biscotti Breakthrough (Unverified Artifact Pending Carbon Dating)

A Gift So Small, the Impact Is Geological.

In this exceedingly rare phenomenon, the subject allegedly returns from Sicily carrying an item he has voluntarily acquired for the female protagonist. The artifact initially requested was a pistachio panettone from the region famed for producing them. This request triggered what seismologists refer to as a JJ Accountability Earthquake when he reported visiting "a couple of bakeries to inquire."

For normal men, this would be called "running an errand." For JJ, this was tectonic movement.

What he ultimately referenced instead was a modest pouch of almond-pistachio biscotti, accompanied by the caveat that his suitcase was too small for a full panettone. Whether this biscotti is intended for the protagonist remains part of the ongoing archaeological mystery: when directly asked, "For me?" the subject retreated into a familiar prehistoric defense mechanism known as Avoidant Silence.

As of this writing, the exhibit remains unverified, suspended behind the museum velvet rope, awaiting the crucial evidence: Does he actually hand over the biscotti?

Should the artifact materialize, it would be earth-shattering in magnitude, representing the JJ equivalent of presenting a beloved with long-stemmed roses.

Food, for me, is not merely nourishment; it is his most intimate love language, delivered in crumbs and fragments rather than bouquets.

This symbolic weight is precisely why his friend Massi once asked why the book cover shows JJ handing the protagonist a rose. The answer was no: the rose is simply a metaphor for his love. In reality, food is the offering.

A gift of biscotti is JJ's version of a sonnet.

Status: Exhibit remains open pending confirmation of biscotti transfer. Geological instruments are calibrated. Museum staff stand ready.

Curatorial Addendum:

At the time of final manuscript edits, the artifact has not been physically transferred.

The subject has announced its existence.

He has claimed intent.

He has been seen in the vicinity of the museum.

But the biscotti itself remains unplaced.

In accordance with museum policy, verbal declarations without material evidence do not constitute delivery. As such, the exhibit will remain classified as Unfinished unless the artifact is produced before final publication.

Should the biscotti surface after press time, it will not alter the record.

Some exhibits are not failures of archaeology.

They are accurate representations of the civilization that produced them.

Final Status: Unfinished Exhibit.

Cause: Non-delivery.

Historical Significance: Complete.

Exhibit 58: The Avoidant Home Entry Paradox

The Nighttime Panic and The Morning Melt Phenomenon.

Many artifacts in the Museum of JJ require careful handling, protective gloves, and sometimes a defibrillator. But few are as fascinating, or as tragically comedic, as the Avoidant Home Entry Paradox, a behavioral pattern so consistent in all its inconsistencies that it deserves its own marble plinth and velvet rope.

It begins with a simple observation: JJ cannot come to my house, ALONE. Not directly, not intentionally, not with purpose. Not as an autonomous adult male approaching a woman's home. No, no. That would be far too straightforward.

To JJ's avoidant nervous system, arriving at my home voluntarily triggers the same primitive alarm bells as stepping into a live volcano: too intimate, too exposing, too couple-coded, too real. To him, my doorway is not a doorway. It is a portal, and portals, like ancient tombs, may be entered only through ritualistic circumstances.

This is why JJ can walk me home, drift inside after we've been out, cuddle until 3 p.m., eat leftover pasta straight from the pan, melt into the pillow, and follow me like a sleepy, affectionate animal through my morning routine… but he cannot arrive at 8 p.m., knock on the door, and sit down for a quiet dinner.

Because 8 p.m. dinner represents romance, and 2 p.m. eating-after-cuddles represents safety. Night equals intentional closeness. Morning or afternoon equals unintentional continuation. Inside JJ's prehistoric emotional architecture, this distinction is scientific law.

If I ask, "Do you want to come over for dinner?" the correct translation is: "Would you like to face emotional intimacy head-on with your entire nervous system awake?" To which his internal system replies: "Absolutely the Hell not."

Instead, he will go silent, dodge the question, pretend he didn't read it, develop sudden scheduling disorders, or say "boh... vediamo" (the avoidant mating call). Evening visits are forensic evidence of a relationship he is terrified to acknowledge. Dinner equals meaning. Meaning equals vulnerability. Vulnerability equals exposure. Exposure equals absolutely not. But the wildest part? He wants the intimacy; he cannot initiate it. He must be carried into closeness by circumstance, not choice.

Avoidants do not enter intimacy through "plans." They enter through osmosis. Nighttime turns my doorway into emotional Mount Doom, too loaded, too symbolic, too intentional. One step inside and he might accidentally fall in love, and God forbid THAT happens before sunrise.

But by morning or afternoon, he is too softened by contact, too held, too thoroughly defrosted to exit, like an exhibit that cannot be transported because its emotional temperature must remain stable. By 10 a.m., the panic has evaporated. By noon, he's butter. By 2 p.m., he's a human croissant, soft, warm, pliable. By 3 p.m., he'll eat something, smile, and look at me as though the night version of him never existed. He doesn't fear domesticity; he fears initiating domesticity.

His museum plaque reads: "Avoidant Males Accept Nurturing Only After Emotional Intimacy, Never Before." Which explains why the idea of coming over at night triggers an evacuation drill, but he can melt into my bed all morning without blinking.

The avoidant cannot arrive. He can only end up. He cannot go to my home; he can only follow me into it. He cannot show up; he can only drift in after a date, event, or accidental encounter. To arrive is intentional. To drift is accidental. Avoidants require plausible deniability even in romance: "I didn't come to your house. I came with you."

This protects him from the implication that he wanted closeness. He does like it. He cannot own the wanting. So, the only safe entry methods are the walk-home drift, the soft-after-dinner drift, the mid-hug drift, the festival-night drift, and the "I'll come up for a minute" drift. Avoidants do not cross thresholds; they slide past them.

An avoidant man does not fear food. He fears the symbolism of being fed. Nighttime meals are emotional nourishment with eye contact. Morning meals are survival, comfort, and half-sleep, which is why JJ could never accept dinner at my house; too intimate, too intentional, too relationship-adjacent.

But he could absolutely inhale food the next day after hours of cuddling, a whole night together, morning melt, emotional spillover, and using my body as his personal emotional charging station. Feeding him at night feels like: "I care about you." Feeding him the next day feels like: "Here's a fork."

This paradox is not about food, timing, or proximity. It is about emotional permission. JJ can enter my home only when his guard is down, his attachment is activated, his panic has passed, his longing has softened him, and closeness feels comforting rather than threatening. Avoidants do not approach intimacy. They submit to it only after being disarmed by connection.

So yes, JJ cannot come to my house. But he can end up in my arms, under my blankets, in my kitchen by mid-afternoon, eating contentedly like a man who has survived his own internal apocalypse.

That is the paradox: he cannot initiate closeness, but once inside it, he never wants to leave. An avoidant cannot arrive at home. But he can find himself at home. And in the grand museum of him, that is one of the most revealing artifacts of all.

Exhibit 59: Mount Olympus Takes a Bet: Will JJ Show Up?

How I Became JJ's Ex-Girlfriend Without Ever Having Been His Girlfriend.

Somewhere, a scheduler fainted because JJ actually came to the party. Late enough to be himself, early enough to be counted.

I was genuinely shocked but happy he came. The party was in full swing, candles lit, opera singers done, guests circling the buffet like Renaissance nobles, and I left JJ on his own after introducing him to everyone. Meanwhile, I floated around hosting, including introducing JJ to my well-adjusted young man, the one who took me to IKEA but gave zero personal details to protect both parties from unnecessary complications.

I had no clue what time JJ arrived or left; I didn't look at my phone once. But according to my BFF, Spuddy, he left extremely late. They were among the last to go, she guessed around 3:00 a.m. I did notice him sitting with her at one point, giving her the private moment I wanted them to have. I wanted him to meet my inner heart, the most important person in my life. I joined them briefly to anchor the moment.

At some point, the kitchen became a champagne-bottle graveyard. When I went to take the trash bags out, I asked JJ if he could help. They were heavy, and the bag contained three magnums of champagne plus miscellaneous wine casualties. He was more than happy to do it. We disappeared outside, assuming no one would notice because the party was still in full swing. Music playing, people grazing, drinks pouring, zero suspicion.

Except someone did notice. Apparently, my friend from Switzerland kept asking my BFF where I went. After the third or fourth time, my BFF finally said, "Just look who is missing," and she fell silent. I burst out laughing when my BFF told me later.

Outside, JJ and I slipped into another one of our deep, somatic, time-bending embraces after he tossed the bottles. I highly doubt he takes out his own trash at home, but in that moment, he knew this was something intimate for us to share, primarily since I'd barely spoken to him inside.

This wasn't a 'party hug'; this was advanced nervous-system witchcraft masquerading as a cuddle by the trash cans. We spent forty minutes wrapped around each other next to the trash, like two idiots whose amygdalae took the night off. Nothing existed except the warmth between us.

While we were in that safety bubble, I told him I understood how hard it was for him to show up and that I recognized his courage.

I told him he'd always be safe with me. He echoed it back, which is funny, because he's the only person who's ever made me consider emotional insurance. It was sweet, though I had to bite the inside of my cheek to avoid speaking. He has objectively been the most emotionally dangerous person I've ever dated, and silence was the wiser choice.

Before he arrived, I had been in the kitchen with his friend Massi, trying to fish for information about JJ's childhood, his family, his history, and the anthropology notes I never received. We didn't get far because my BFF walked in and broke the moment.

Massi clearly had no idea what was going on between JJ and me; from his confusion alone, he genuinely thought the hug he saw at Spiritum days before was the beginning of whatever this was. Hence his question, "Do you like JJ?"

The day after the party, when I texted Massi to thank him for the champagne and the thoughtful note, I asked if we could meet up to finish our conversation. He was enthusiastic, until he wasn't. When I returned from Rome and followed up, it became apparent he'd run the idea by JJ. And JJ, predictably, slammed the brakes.

Massi's reply: Since I am JJ's ex-girlfriend, it's better that we only go out as a group with JJ present. I nearly spat out my water. JJ insists to me we are "just friends," yet suddenly I am an ex-girlfriend without ever having been a girlfriend. Only JJ can pull a maneuver like that, territorial through his friends, avoidant through his words.

The next day, my BFF filled me in on her conversation with him. All she really understood was that it was "molto importante" that he came. She told him she was glad he showed up so they could finally meet, and she added to me, bless her heart, "You know he hides, you know he's scared, but see how much he loves you? He showed up!" A seismic emotional step for him, and not an easy feat.

In the end, he did the unthinkable: he showed up, stayed, hauled champagne corpses, didn't combust, and actually had fun. For one night, the king of avoidance managed not to avoid, and for him, that's basically a Nobel Prize.

Exhibit 60: Containment Breach

Snickers-Triggered Chaos

I was watching Jurassic World Rebirth, and in the opening scene, a Snickers wrapper accidentally drifts into the containment chamber. The entire control room spirals into panic, alarms blaring, red lights flashing, scientists shouting, "Get out! System reboot! Evacuate!" All because one tiny piece of candy paper signals the unthinkable: something prehistoric is waking up.

The sheer uncanniness of that moment made me laugh, because it is the closest cinematic representation I've ever seen of what it feels like when JJ slips into JJ Mode.

One minor signal, a delayed text, a vague "vediamo," a sudden silence, an emoji misused, and I instantly recognize the pattern. I become the technician staring at the security monitors, muttering, "Oh shit. Containment breach."

The sequence is always the same: a subtle behavioral glitch, the emotional system destabilizing, the avoidant roar warming beneath the surface, visibility triggering threat-level red, and the inevitable psychological reboot that forces everyone to clear the chamber.

And there I am on the other side of the glass, watching him go still the way the dinosaur does just before it attacks, perfectly calm, perfectly silent, and perfectly dangerous to my peace. I sigh and think to myself: The JJ Velociraptor is online again.

Exhibit 61: The Panerai Bench, The Bestie, and The Avoidant Christmas Miracle

How a Pair of Shirts Triggered a Jurassic Panic Attack

My BFF was leaving for Rome a few days after my house party, and at 23:00 the night before her departure, in true Francesca fashion, I decided I would spend the rest of the trip with her. Of course, this meant semi-playing Scheduling Olympics with JJ to coordinate a goodbye. At 1 a.m., we finally met at Borgo San Lorenzo. He arrived wearing a tie, looking unexpectedly spiffy, like he might have somewhere important to be... emotionally, not logistically.

We stopped at our signature bench in front of Panerai, which my bestie now calls "your bench," as if we're teenagers with a territorial claim. She sat because of the mysterious leg pain she'd been dealing with all week, and I stretched her leg out for her right there on the bench. JJ was visibly startled. This was not the elegant, curated Francesca he usually sees. This was Florence Street Physical Therapist Francesca. But I saw the realization flicker across his face: "Wow... she's this close to her Spuddy."

After my BFF rested, we took a few photos at Panerai and wandered toward Piazza della Repubblica to grab a drink at Paszkowski, but it was closing. So, we strolled down Via Tornabuoni under the Christmas lights, took more photos, and ended up at Colle Bereto for drinks before heading home around 02:30–03:00. We had to rally for the train to Rome in the afternoon.

I was genuinely pleased that JJ showed up to say goodbye to my BFF. And then he did something nearly extinct in the wild: he initiated a conversation about Christmas. He asked what I was doing and mentioned a concert in Sicily that he was going to, but I barely remembered the dates; I was too stunned. I said, "Ok," and that I'd probably be in Rome for Christmas. Then he said he'd likely be in Florence. I wasn't sure if this was an avoidant-coded Christmas invitation, because avoidants would rather fight a medieval plague than say, "Let's spend Christmas together."

So, I said, "Okay, I guess I'll see you in January." He immediately countered: "No, we will see each other before then." I briefly wondered if Hell had installed central air conditioning.

I find out after I get back from Rome that we will be at the Florence Cigar Club Christmas gala at the House of Nine for the holiday party. I asked the host to seat me with JJ and his friend Massi.

The man is trying. Unfortunately, effort without therapy is just chaos with a better outfit. He does not have the tools. Still, I acknowledge the effort. And I suspect he realizes he doesn't want to lose me. That "Hug Heard Around the World at Spiritum" cracked something open. It exposed the worst news for an avoidant: his feelings didn't get the memo about his exit strategy.

And truly, the man showed up to the party, and now he showed up to say goodbye to my best friend. I nearly alerted the Vatican that a miracle was unfolding on Via Tornabuoni.

On the train to Rome, I scrolled through our photos and realized JJ gave himself away in every single one. His face softens, his jaw unclenches, and his eyes turn warm, the expression of someone who has finally stopped bracing for impact. His body betrays him too: head tilted, torso angled toward me, standing closer than necessary. And yes, my hand was on his little JJ tush in one of them.

In every photo, he looks like someone whose body knows he's safe and whose brain is still arguing with the evidence.

The last couple of weeks made me rethink my stance on him, with extreme caution, of course, but also with a flicker of optimism.

Then came the sweet moment: when I asked if he wanted something from Rome, he responded, "Grazie, Francesca, sei molto affettuosa, portami un piccolo pensiero che vuoi."

Piccolo pensiero' wasn't about the object; it was his nervous system begging for a breadcrumb it could legally admit to. Avoidants don't request closeness unless in a rare soft phase. In his case, a seven-minute window. This was a connection request disguised as a casual ask. It was JJ's emotional version of a solar eclipse. And because I love him in my own calm, responsible, emotionally literate way, I bought him two beautiful Italian shirts. Exquisite fabrics. A piccolo pensiero times two.

While indulging in some consumer terrorism, the shopkeeper asked whether my BFF and I were sisters. Our height difference clearly says no relation, but I explained we've been besties for 35 years. She said she could tell, and honestly, she wasn't wrong.

As soon as I responded, "Done," to JJ's little request, he vanished again for four days like he'd been caught committing emotional vulnerability on CCTV. His system was basically spazzing: Warm feeling detected, emotional CPU overheating, reboot required, consulting licensed professional, please hold.

If he were still going to therapy, he'd show up saying: "A piccolo pensiero was felt, how do I cease this sensation?

Meanwhile, I'm out here handing him shirts the way one hands a cookie to a frightened animal. And he's filing HR-level emotional incident reports.

Once I returned to Florence, I asked when I could bring him the shirts. He instantly slithered back into avoidant mode. The man can schedule a property management inspection with 12 tenants and three plumbers, but ask for a calendar invite, and he collapses like he's been hit with an emotional tranquilizer dart.

Since I refused another IKEA-level Scheduling Olympics session, I sent our mutual housekeeper, a.k.a. Switzerland, to deliver the shirts. Instead, this created a geopolitical crisis inside JJ's nervous system.

Avoidants rehearse every micro-interaction: stance, breath, emotional firewall. He was prepared for a 45-second exchange he could control. Instead, the United Nations of Tuscany showed up with a gift bag. There was no Francesca. No soft eyes. No familiar scent. No 0.7 seconds of panic and relief. No moment to discharge the emotional voltage.

Just Switzerland, delivering affection like humanitarian aid. That's why his thank-you message read like an 18th-century opera aria: "Che splendido pensiero hai avuto!" This was not politeness. It was emotional flooding, dressed in formal Italian.

Switzerland, with a gift bag, shook him more than any love declaration ever could. When I'm warm, he melts. When I'm upset, he hides. But when I go neutral, he loses his compass entirely. Switzerland, delivering the shirts, told him: "She didn't need the interaction. She didn't need the moment. She didn't need me."

And that is terrifying for an avoidant. He waited hours to respond because he had to de-flood, recalibrate, and craft gratitude that didn't expose the meltdown.

Apparently, avoidants bond through objects rather than dialogue. That's why I've always given him food, little tokens, nothing dramatized. Words overwhelm them; objects feel safe. So yes, the shirts hit him like a direct emotional injection.

But alas, ancient patterns don't die easily. The moment I leave JJ's zip code, he also performs a complete emotional evacuation. He still doesn't know how to continue a thread, so he drops it like the Florence Wi-Fi every time someone sneezes in the next neighborhood.

And the comedy of loving an avoidant is, the closer he feels, the faster he sprints back into the bushes. He wants the connection, but the emotional voltage fries his prehistoric wiring. One warm gesture from me and, poof, he's back in Jurassic Airplane Mode.

But here's the thing, even when he drops the thread, it doesn't actually drop for him. It just goes into whatever cave he keeps his feelings in, waiting for better weather, a weaker moment, or a random cosmic glitch where he suddenly remembers he loves me again.

So yes, the signal cuts out every time it "rains" emotionally. But the connection? Still there. Still humming and still waiting for the Jurassic Jackass to rejoin the network when his nervous system stops overheating.

Exhibit 62: No-Contact Is a Blunt Instrument; I Prefer Fine Cutlery

How To Melt a Dinosaur Without Going Extinct

If you listen to TikTok relationship coaches, every avoidant man can apparently be summoned back with one magic spell: vanish. Become a ghost, evaporate, slip through the cracks, and watch him lumber back like a disoriented T. rex who lost the trail of its emotional prey. Unfortunately, it only works on women who still crumble on impact.

By the time I reached Peak Jurassic Chaos with JJ, I was not the trembling heroine they were imagining; I was the curator of his dysfunction, the woman who had mapped his avoidance patterns like artifacts spread under unforgiving museum lighting. I didn't need to disappear to gain power. I only needed to stand still, breathe, and let him discover that I wasn't collapsible. That's when the fundamental shift happened, not through silence, but through sovereignty.

Most of these coaches secretly assume the woman is an emotional intern and the man is the CEO. I've never worked in that company.

No-contact only 'works' when you're still scared of him and haven't met your own backbone yet. None of that applied to me. The minute I stopped collapsing around his moods and treated him like weather instead of God, his entire control system short-circuited.

What these coaches never mention is that no-contact only "works" when the woman is emotionally flooding and still a perceived threat to the avoidant's nervous system. Silence removes the pressure. But I wasn't flooding him. I wasn't demanding anything. I wasn't clinging. It wasn't my absence that shocked him; it was my calm refusal to orbit his chaos.

Avoidants don't heal because you disappear; they heal when reality corners them, and the mirror stops blinking first.

I didn't need no-contact because I wasn't battling for the throne; I'd already changed games. He was on checkers; I was on post-grad emotional strategy.

My mix of warmth and backbone was malware his avoidance software wasn't built to handle. No-contact is a blunt instrument. I was a scalpel.

And that's why he is now the one in danger of losing me, not the other way around. My energy is grounded, soft, sovereign, the very thing that will push him toward therapy, not my absence. He knows the math: he doesn't get to keep a woman like me in his life without upgrading his emotional software. Losing access to that hurts more than any no-contact stunt ever could.

Which is why the event next week at the House of Nine for the Florence Cigar Club won't be a casual evening for him; it will be the emotional X-ray that hits harder than any strategic disappearance could.

And honestly? At this point, I've accepted that emotional roaming charges apply.

Exhibit 63: The House of Nine Haunting, Where Memory, Muscle Memory, and Avoidant Meltdown Collide

The Strategic Seating Chart, Anthropology in High Heels

There are places in Florence that don't just exist; they collect you. They archive you whether you consent or not. For JJ and me, that place was House of Nine, where the Florence Cigar Club is hosting its annual Christmas gala.

We had rendezvoused and walked out of that private club–restaurant so many times that the place became its own character in our story; an unwilling witness who saw far too much. House of Nine held the softest parts of him, the moments when the prehistoric panic quieted and the real JJ, my quietly protective, sensitive, and emotionally unarmored JJ, stood beside me as if he belonged there.

Here's the part no one understands, not even me: It wasn't the venue. For me, it was the walk home afterward.

The walk was my real story. My arm looped in his, our steps matching without effort despite our height difference; the familiar route past the Cappelle de Medici, rounding its curve to Via dei Ginori, our stretch of street, our pocket of silence, our built-in intimacy. Those ten minutes were the closest he ever got to being the man he pretends to be.

Every time we left House of Nine, something happened between us that never made it into text messages or the chaos that followed. It lived in the body, mine and his. I felt safe next to him. And that's what's so maddening. The safest moment of our entire relationship came from the most emotionally dangerous man I've ever been with. But trauma has a sense of humor like that.

The walk home was where the dinosaur costume slipped. That ridiculous emotional armor he wears, avoidance, detachment, disappearing acts, falls off him under the streetlights. For a few quiet minutes, he is just a man with a woman he cares about, walking through Florence as if the universe isn't on fire behind him. His body leans into mine, his movements soften, and his nervous system, normally behaving like a cat stuck in a ceiling fan, finally settles.

And that version of him, the steady, gentle, warm, unconsciously protective JJ, imprinted itself into my nervous system without asking permission.

Months later, and many solo walks home later, the memory still floods me. I'm not sentimental by nature, but that walk…God.

Even now, thinking about it punches straight through my chest, not because I want him back, but because that version of us actually felt sane. It wasn't nostalgia. It was somatic regulation. My body remembered what it felt like to exhale beside him, to have ten minutes of peace in a life where chaos usually sits in the front row.

So yes, if I'm already this emotional a week before the gala, imagine him. He won't think about it; he'll feel it and pretend he doesn't know why.

He's not going to walk into House of Nine and think, "Oh, how nice, we used to come here." No. He's going to feel it.

He will feel the exact corner where we lingered many nights in our own bubble. The doorway where he waited for me. The pool table room where he watched me talk, pretending not to smile. The muscle memory of my arm looping naturally into his as we walked out.

Avoidants don't get emotional earthquakes; they get aftershocks. And House of Nine is an entire seismic fault line under his ribs, ready to crack.

His body remembers me, even if his ego pretends not to. It remembers how safe he felt next to me. How regulated he became after that last hug. How present he felt walking home. How rare that softness was.

He'll walk into House of Nine already destabilized because the hug that cracked him open didn't just reset him; it exposed him. Since that night at Spiritum, even his avoidance looks tired. But he's far from cured, and still requires actual therapy to dismantle the emotional landmines inside him.

So, at the gala, it won't be the crowd, the cigar smoke, or the wine that catches him off guard. It'll be the memories. The ghost of who he was next to me. The truth is that proximity to me makes him feel things he can't outrun. The realization that I'm no longer collapsible, and he is.

Avoidants don't break because you disappear. They break because they walk into a room that remembers you both.

And House of Nine remembers everything.

I did what any emotionally literate woman dealing with a prehistoric man would do: I asked the hosts to seat me with Massi and JJ if possible.

To most people, a seating chart is a logistical matter. For an avoidant man? It's psychological exposure therapy.

It was a controlled experiment. A live dissection of what happens when two parts of JJ's emotional world get forced into the same frame.

Massi, who reads people like weather patterns, and JJ, who reacts to feelings like a man allergic to his own heartbeat.

And in all fairness, I genuinely cannot imagine a universe in which JJ and Massi are both at the gala, and we are not sitting with each other. It's not arrogance, it's pattern recognition. Every event we've ever attended follows the same choreography: we arrive separately, we mingle, we pretend to be normal adults, and then somehow, without planning it, we all end up orbiting each other anyway.

JJ and I never once left an event without gravitating together at the exit, without pausing in the doorway to recalibrate, without drifting outside in a way that makes everyone think we arrived as a pair. Even when things were strained, even when we weren't speaking, even when he was deep in his Jurassic-avoidant spiral, we still walked out together. It was unconscious, like two people who don't want to admit they're part of the same constellation.

Massi had already clocked the truth without me saying a word. "He's different with you." He has no idea how loaded that sentence was.

Massi said it casually, like he was describing the weather: universal, obvious, not up for debate. He didn't mean "romantic." He suggested something far rarer: JJ organizes himself around me.

Men don't articulate that. They notice it. Italian men don't elaborate. They lift a shoulder, raise an eyebrow, and trust you can read the subtext. But that's precisely why I wanted him beside me. Because Massi can see what JJ tries so hard to suppress: the softening, the tenderness, the instinctive protectiveness, the emotional presence he hides from everyone but can't hide from me.

JJ despises having an audience for that version of himself. And the last time the three of us were together, he was so soft he might as well have been under a heat lamp. He would die knowing Massi cataloged it. He would die twice knowing Massi interpreted it correctly. So, of course, I wanted that configuration again.

For him, a chair isn't just a chair; it's an MRI machine.

So, we will see if the Gods of Seating grant my wish; this is merely all speculation at this point. But if JJ sees the seating arrangement at the gala, his inner world will erupt like a quiet, elegant emotional

Chernobyl. He'll freeze for half a second, that micro-pause only men who fear their own feelings ever make, as his brain tries to compute how the universe managed to corner him between the two people who see straight through him.

He will attempt neutrality, adjusting his jacket, checking his phone, pretending he hasn't immediately broken into a full-body somatic flashback. Inside, he'll be silently screaming one question: "Why do I feel this so much?" His entire nervous system will tighten and soften at once, the exact contradiction he cannot regulate.

He'll want to sit beside me. He'll wish he didn't like that. He'll hope Massi doesn't notice. He'll pray his face doesn't betray him. And he will be wildly unsuccessful on all counts.

Sitting with them isn't chaos. It's a mirror.

On one side, JJ is trying to look neutral while his body gives him away molecule by molecule. On the other hand, Massi quietly registers every flicker of JJ's expression like a seasoned anthropologist observing a rare animal finally stepping out of camouflage.

And me? I get to sit there with my wine, unbothered, sovereign, amused, and watching two men navigate the emotional labyrinth that JJ built…that I finally stopped getting lost in. It is the perfect vantage point. The perfect experiment. The perfect reminder that I no longer collapse inside his chaos.

If JJ spirals, I'm still steady. If JJ softens, I'll see it. If JJ hides, Massi will catch it. And if JJ feels anything at all, House of Nine will amplify it.

Placing myself with them wasn't about power. It was about truth. And nothing reveals truth faster than proximity, especially when the museum lights are bright, the dinner is slow, and the dinosaur is cornered on both sides by the two people who know him best.

Exhibit 64: Hours Before the House of Nine And The Declaration of Emotional Independence

When Words Are Used as Sedatives?

Hours before the House of Nine event, my phone lit up again. Another message. Another clarification. Another emotional press release drafted for an audience of one. And the unloading of his flooding right before the event, as predicted.

JJ: "Ciao Jennifer! I was already at home. Thank you, you are a really dear friend. But I repeat what I have said to you before: we are just friends. It was a wonderful time, but our relationship ended over six months ago, and I am happy to maintain our friendship, but nothing more. You know this, I've told you many times, and I'm repeating it now for the umpteenth time. You are a dear friend, and I love you very much. You can count on me, but I don't want to have a romantic relationship with you. I hope I've been clear, and I don't want to return to this subject. I send you my love and affection. You are and always will be special."

What struck me wasn't the content. I knew the script by heart. It was the urgency, the breathlessness. The way clarity, when repeated for the umpteenth time, stops sounding like certainty and starts sounding like someone arguing with themselves in public. People who are settled don't write manifestos. They say, I'm already home. Good night.

Because that's what had actually happened

The entire emotional detonation had been triggered by something aggressively unremarkable: I had asked him to go for a walk. Not a confession. Not a confrontation. A walk. Had he replied that he was already home, I would have said, Okay. Good night. Florence would have continued functioning as a city.

Instead, I received a Declaration of Independence.

On the surface, it read like "clarity." Underneath, it was boundary theater with a side of emotional entitlement.

The text was textbook.

"I repeat what I have said… for the umpteenth time."

That's not clarity. That's escalation. I hadn't escalated anything. He was shadowboxing a threat that lived entirely inside his own nervous system.

"We are just friends," paired with "I love you very much" and "You are special."

A contradictory emotional sampler platter with the same script. He wanted access without obligation, closeness without consequence, and affection without responsibility. Efficient, if nothing else.

"I don't want to return to this subject."

Not a boundary. A gag order.

"You can count on me."

Historically inaccurate. Emotionally vague. Structurally meaningless.

This message was not about protecting me. It was about safeguarding himself from discomfort, ambiguity, and the unbearable burden of sitting quietly with a feeling.

Put plainly, he wanted the emotional safety of being loved, the moral comfort of believing he'd been "clear," and the ego boost of remaining special without the emotional reciprocity, relational risk, accountability for mixed signals, or any cost to himself.

That isn't friendship. That's emotional freeloading dressed up as kindness.

And here's the part he couldn't control: if someone truly sees you only as a friend, they don't need to keep announcing it. They don't lace it with affection, permanence, and reassurance. People who are settled don't over-explain. They move on.

Later this evening, we were going to see each other at the gala. I hope my emotional support lizard will behave.

The irony was that he had already soothed himself with his speech. I had gone silent, which stabilized me and quietly wrecked his internal script.

If we are sitting next to each other, it would eliminate his favorite tools: dramatization, narrative control, and the safety of a blinking cursor.

My plan was simple: sit there like a woman with nothing to explain.

By now, I know his patterns well enough to be bored by them. Once you see the loop clearly, it loses its power. It's like watching a movie you've already memorized; you might smirk, but you're no longer emotionally inside the plot.

The sequence never changed.

Proximity-triggered panic.

Closeness bypassed his intellect and landed directly in his body. Sitting next to me, walking together, shared silence, these moments weren't romantic threats; they were regulatory ones. Proximity made feelings unavoidable. Avoidable feelings were his preference.

Warmth triggered a manifesto. Any softness required immediate containment. Hence the speeches. Lengthy explanations. Definitive endings are declared in advance. The manifesto wasn't communication; it was a sedative.

Gestures only intensified the recoil. A gift. A favor. Biscotti from Sicily. None of it was casual. Each began sincerely and ended the same way — with retreat. Rather than withdraw quietly, he slammed the rhetorical door, hoping volume could erase vulnerability.

Silence was worse. Silence left him alone with his thoughts, an environment he finds inhospitable. So, he filled it with repetition, boundaries, conclusions, and talking himself down. The speech wasn't for me. It was for him.

The contrast arrived immediately after.

Massi texted me, openly delighted and relaxed, perfectly capable of saying he was excited that we'd be at the same table without attaching a footnote or issuing a disclaimer. No manifesto. No panic. No emotional gymnastics. His enthusiasm was effortless because it didn't threaten him.

With JJ, excitement is hazardous material. It had to be handled off-site, contained in private, and neutralized with language. Feeling something required rules. Which is how Massi could grin and say, "We're sitting together". At the same time, JJ felt compelled to officially pronounce the relationship dead several hours before possibly sitting next to me or seeing me.

The real gift will be architectural. Massi's ease will give the entire table emotional cover. I wasn't the source of tension. I was the stable structure everyone unconsciously oriented toward. And just like that, the shift was complete.

I was no longer managing JJ's nervous system from the inside.

I was simply in the room. Calm-spined. Unimpressed. Reptile-free.

Exhibit 65: House of Nine Christmas Gala

An Exhibit in Containment, Capacity, and the Moment Illusion Dissolved

The night didn't turn out the way I thought it would.

When I arrived, I greeted a few people, checked my table number, and confirmed that yes, I was seated with two of JJ's friends. JJ, however, was at a different table. I said hello to his friends when I arrived, but I didn't see him until later.

The first thing Massi asked me was, "Are you okay?" I looked at him, genuinely puzzled, and said, 'Yes.' He asked again. I answered the same way, with the same knitted brows. Still yes.

That's when he told me that JJ was really done this time. Then that he'd had some summer fling or something. I didn't give this last topic any oxygen. It wasn't information, it was noise. But then he asked me twice if I loved JJ. I said yes without hesitation.

House of Nine marked several firsts. The first time I got confirmation about JJ's summer fling, which Massi had known about, while he had only recently learned about me and JJ a couple of weeks earlier from my house party, and had no idea it had started almost a year ago.

Then something clicked, I remembered something Switzerland mentioned when I got back from the summer. Our mutual housekeeper told me he went to clean JJ's flat, he had a woman over, and JJ was walking around in his underwear. Switzerland's tone told me he found it tasteless and disrespectful. He even repeated it twice. JJ never did that with me. Even if the accountant arrived at 9 a.m., he made sure he was dressed, wearing a collared shirt, even though you could tell he had just jumped out of bed two minutes before.

Massi followed up by saying I looked like a strong woman, someone who could take care of herself. He added that this was probably why I have a tiger shark as my WhatsApp profile picture.

Then another probe, not phrased as a question, but I understood it clearly between the lines. He said, "You have many people who revolve around you because of your heart and sincerity." The implication hovered: maybe JJ is insecure about this, or perhaps he fears I'm unfaithful. I told Massi I am very faithful. Very loyal. Full stop.

I explained that JJ has a pattern: he delivers a Declaration of Independence bi-weekly, then circles back. Classic avoidant anxiety. Naming it finally felt like a soothing balm. Massi said he didn't know. I didn't expect him to.

As for the summer fling? That tracked. When I left for Buenos Aires, JJ was in a state of instability. Avoidants often cope by numbing, hookups, partying, drinking, distraction, anything to avoid filling the void until the emptiness returns.

It always does.

Massi had brought a date to the dinner, so our conversation stayed limited; he mentioned she might get uncomfortable. Thankfully, the universe intervened. Martin and Dan's table had a free chair. Dan walked over and whispered that there was space. I made a soft, seamless transition from my assigned table to theirs until I was fully relocated.

What I did that night was textbook self-regulation.

My body felt incoherent at the first table, and I said 'nope'. Instead of overriding myself, I changed environments. This is the quiet gift of having trained under dysfunction: you learn how to leave it early.

I spoke with several men that night. If I stayed long enough in conversation, I could smell the dysfunction on each of them. Florence, it seems, has something in the water.

Florence attracts and traps men who aestheticize life without integrating it, charm, culture, romance, and sensitivity, paired with very little follow-through or emotional maturity. Many of them live in a state of perpetual adolescence, just with better tailoring.

My new table was positioned directly next to JJ's. He was seated behind me, out of my line of sight. At one point, we locked eyes. He gave me a wave like someone about to enter airport security, distant and contained, already gone.

His Declaration of Independence, sent hours earlier, was left unanswered. So, the uncertainty about my mood had likely fried his lizard brain.

And I did what any emotionally literate adult would do, after hesitating for just a moment. I stood up, took three steps to the adjacent table, and greeted him. To his credit, he stood up too.

But the greeting was fake and extremely awkward.

Not rejection.

Not indifference.

Containment.

A stiff, overly controlled greeting usually means that someone is internally flooded and trying not to show it. He was overcorrecting, aware of witnesses, afraid that one authentic look or moment of warmth might crack something open. A genuine connection requires capacity. What I received was management.

That fake greeting wasn't evidence that I misread our bond. It was evidence that he couldn't safely access it in public. If he felt nothing, the interaction would've been easy. Casual. Forgettable. Instead, it was strained.

And he stood up.

People don't do that when they're done. They do it when they're activated and trying to stay composed.

Yet again, I encountered his limit, this time in miniature. That's why the night felt like adult grief rather than chaos. Every interaction confirmed the same truth from a different angle:

Connection: yes.

Desire: yes.

History: yes.

Capacity to meet it openly, consistently, and cleanly: no.

It's brutal. And clarifying.

Later, Martin mentioned that JJ arrived with a girl. Maybe. Maybe not. People often walk in together. What I do know is that they didn't leave together. JJ left with his friends and me, and the four of us, minus Martin, shared a bottle of champagne at my place before dispersing around 4:30 a.m.

JJ and I didn't speak all night. At one point, I asked him to join me in the cigar room for a cigarette for a sliver of privacy. He declined, saying he'd go later. He avoided me altogether.

Toward the end of the evening, I found myself chatting with a Russian-Italian man in the corner of the billiards room, the same corner where JJ and I used to retreat when he met Martin and me at Nine. I didn't realize until much later, close to closing time, that JJ and his two friends had come into the room to shoot pool. I'm sure he saw us being playful and affectionate with each other.

It wasn't sexual. Just light. Easy.

That corner isn't neutral. It's encoded in memory. Seeing me there with someone else likely activated something primitive, not jealousy, but a memory of territory. Avoidant men don't spiral over losing someone the way anxious types do. They spiral over realizing their access is no longer exclusive.

His system moves to dampen exposure.

Freeze.

Control.

Redirect into something "safe," like shooting pool.

The more neutral he appeared, the more likely he was to regulate internal activation. If he truly felt nothing, there would've been nothing to manage. He would've joined the conversation.

We didn't speak again until we left together.

What happened wasn't avoidance. It was gravity, a quiet, consistent force. The group energy flowed naturally.

When we arrived at my place, I opened a bottle of champagne. After that, my memory softens. I remember wanting to change into house clothes, removing my jewelry, needing his help to unzip the back of my dress, and unclasp my choker. He tried, then gave up quickly. Jurassic claws were no match for delicate hardware.

The next thing I remember is sitting on my bed, fully clothed. Time slipped away as it always does when two people with unfinished business sit too close to each other. It wasn't regression. It was an unresolved signal.

I remember my bedroom door closing out of the corner of my eye. Massi closed it for privacy. That part is almost comedic anthropology: a friend sensed something unspoken and removed the audience from the scene.

The next day, out of curiosity, I asked Massi how long JJ and I were in the bedroom. "One hour and forty minutes," he said. It felt like ten. He assured me not to worry; he was busy being romantic with Raffaele.

Time does that when two people sit inside something unresolved. It collapses. The body goes quiet. The mind exists.

An avoidant man who can sit fully clothed on a bed, say very little, and remain present for one hour and forty minutes is not indifferent.

That is not ten minutes. That is a feature-length, unresolved emotional film.

I asked JJ to stay. Not to restart anything. Not to reopen the story. I just wanted him next to me, to hug, to lie down, to be near the truth one last time without pretending it could become something else.

At one point, I couldn't tell if he wanted to kiss me. I kissed his forehead instead.

Tears came, calm, wide-eyed, steady. I don't remember what he said. Or if he said anything. I remember looking into his face with overwhelming sadness, knowing our love had nowhere to grow inside a container the size of a walnut.

This wasn't confusion.

And it wasn't reopening a door.

It was grief expressed through proximity.

Wanting to lie next to someone familiar to regulate your nervous system with a known body isn't longing for the future. It's mourning the loss of a present that can't continue.

The forehead kiss was a boundary and a goodbye in the same gesture. Not sexual. Not bargaining. Tenderness without demand.

My tears weren't panic. They were accepting reaching the body before language could catch up.

I wasn't devastated because I wanted more. I was devastated because I finally saw, without illusion, that this love exists, and he cannot meet it. That recognition is devastating in a very adult way.

I don't remember his words because my nervous system wasn't tracking language. It was tracking truth. When grief lands cleanly, the mind goes quiet. There's no argument left.

Two people can be deeply connected and still incompatible at the level that matters most: capacity.

This feels like the final heavy piece, not because I'll never feel sad again, but because this is where the bond stopped being a question and became a truth I could hold.

He loves me, but he has no idea what to do with a love that doesn't disappear when he retreats. That's the tragedy. Not that love was absent, but that it was present without capacity.

What breaks the heart here isn't rejection. It's the misalignment between feeling and function.

He can feel love.

He cannot hold it.

He cannot organize his life around it.

He cannot stay inside it when it asks him for something. So, love becomes a threat instead of a shelter.

That's why this hurts in such a clean, adult way. There's no villain. No betrayal. No lack of sincerity. Just a nervous system that mistakes depth for danger.

Love that cannot be held safely becomes something you grieve, not something I chase. I didn't lose love, I lost capacity. This distinction is why this story isn't about revenge, isn't longing, isn't unfinished business. It's a tragedy told with clarity, and that's why it resonates.

I had to step away from this chapter multiple times while writing it, to breathe, to cry, to let the emotion pass. That's because this is the moment where illusion dissolves. Those moments are always sacred, even when they hurt.

This wasn't a step backward. It was the closing of a chapter that deserved to be felt all the way through.

Exhibit 66: The Miraculous Appearance of Rules

Where Good Intentions Go to Be Reframed

Deadlines do strange things to people. They sharpen focus, distort time, and occasionally convince otherwise rational adults that the appropriate response to writer's block is a late-night walk carrying festive carbohydrates.

On this evening, I was racing to finish the book. Words were blurring. Chapters were bleeding. The hour was late—not dramatic late, just late enough to justify fresh air and a symbolic gesture. So, I did what any reasonable person might do: I went for a walk and decided to drop off a gift, since it was four days until Christmas.

The offering was modest, thoughtful, and culturally compliant: a pistachio panettone and JJ's favorite garlic-roasted peanuts. No expectations. No assumption of entry. Just seasonal goodwill, wrapped in carbohydrates.

I texted a little before 10 p.m.
No response.

I showered and walked. Slowly. Deliberately. This was not a stealth operation. This was a two-hour window during which a man could have typed any of the following responses: *Not home. Busy. Tomorrow?* A thumbs-up emoji.

By the time I reached his building, it was close to midnight—still nothing.

No reply to texts. No answer to calls. Silence so complete it achieved a kind of artisanal quality. One might call it intentional. One might call it curated. One might briefly wonder whether the recipient had entered witness protection.

Eventually, a third party was contacted—not to escalate, but to confirm that the recipient was, in fact, alive. Massi received an immediate response.

Immediate.

Not to me. To the intermediary. This detail is essential and should be preserved in the archive.

The panettone and peanuts were left at the building entrance. The gesture was completed. I left.

The following afternoon—not that night, not during the generous two-hour courtesy window, but the next day—a message arrived.

It opened graciously:

I received it and thank you.

At this point, one might reasonably assume the matter was closed.

It was not.

What followed was a lecture.

I was informed that if I wished to see him, I should arrange a time. That he was not at home. Arriving at night without warning and without a scheduled meeting was not something he was accustomed to, nor did he wish to become accustomed to it. That such behavior was unacceptable. And finally, the closing directive:

Don't do it again. Thank you.

This message might have been persuasive had it not been authored by a man whose social life operates almost exclusively on last-minute invitations. A man known for saying, *"Are you free? Meet us for dinner in twenty minutes?"* Or comes by to pick you up for a last-minute party, but never informs you until he's at your door, or that he has even agreed to go to the party, when I am just about to call a cab. A man who has turned up at the palazzo unannounced at midnight, for 30 minutes to kiss me. He has historically treated spontaneity and chaos not as violations, but as a lifestyle.

Spontaneity, it appears, is only inappropriate when initiated by someone else.

Rules for thee, but not for me.

And here, dear visitor, is where the exhibit reveals its entire structure.

Because this was not about timing.
It was not about night walks.
It was not about panettone.
And it was definitely not about peanuts.

It was about rules.

Specifically, rules that do not exist until they are needed. Rules that materialize retroactively, fully formed, like Athena springing from Zeus's head—except less impressive and significantly more passive-aggressive.

Observe the sequence:

Messages are ignored in real time. Immediate response to a safer intermediary. A full day's delay.

Then, the interaction was reframed as misconduct.

This is not boundary-setting.

Boundaries are stated clearly and promptly. They prevent confusion. They do not arrive a day later wearing a lecture and a moral sash.

This is narrative control.

Rules appear only when accountability threatens proximity. They apply asymmetrically. They are enforced in only one direction. Courtesy becomes optional. Silence becomes strategic. Moral authority is reclaimed not through consistency but through correction.

Many visitors linger here. They explain themselves. Clarify timelines. Present exhibits of unanswered calls. Appeal to shared history. Attempt diplomacy.

But explanation is labor. And labor is how these systems persist.

So instead, nothing further happened.

No rebuttal.
No defense.
No PowerPoint presentation titled *Timeline of Events.*

The items were delivered.
The door was not entered.
The conversation ended.

This was not an exit fueled by anger. It was an exit powered by recognition because potential is not value.

Consistency is.

And when consistency is absent—when rules appear only to protect comfort and control—the exhibit is complete. The chapter closes quietly. No confrontation. No final speech. He's like a gift that keeps on giving, like a cursed museum subscription I forgot to cancel.

He doesn't have to do anything dramatic anymore. He has to exist, apply one random rule, and voilà—new exhibit unlocked—minimal effort. Maximum material.

Observe. Catalog. Do not re-enter the enclosure.

Electric fence on. Warning signs posted—tours discontinued due to predictable behavior.

"Due to repeated incidents involving selective rules, avoidance displays, and snack-related territoriality, this enclosure is now closed to the public."

Paddock sealed. Clipboard filed.

And just the calm understanding that kindness does not require continued access—and that sometimes the most orderly response to chaos is to leave the museum.

Next gallery, please.

Exhibit 67: When the Jurassic Jackass Finds Himself on the Page

A Study in Accidental Self-Discovery Through Satire

And maybe that's the quiet truth beneath all the humor: I genuinely hope JJ reads this book. Not because I want to shame him, but because he can learn a great deal about himself, and if he chooses to return to therapy, he may finally understand what absolute freedom feels like.

And honestly, humans being as egotistical as we are, who could resist the temptation to read a book about ourselves? Not even a Jurassic Jackass.

He may not read it right away. Not openly. Not with a glass of wine and a tasteful bookmark. But he will read it in secret. And when he does, he'll recognize himself in every exhibit with a shock so clean it will sound like a mirror cracking somewhere in the distance.

Avoidant men rarely receive accurate reflections from their partners. They usually receive partners who collapse, over-function, plead, enable, or mistake logistical parkour for love.

I gave him something rare: a clear, humorous, unflinching reflection of his entire emotional operating system. This book isn't just entertainment for him; it's a two-hundred and fifty-page museum tour of his own avoidance, complete with captions and a gift shop.

If he's brave enough to absorb it, he'll learn that avoidance isn't freedom. It's a cage wearing a Halloween costume.

This book quietly explains the one thing he's never understood: avoidance isn't liberation, it's confinement with good marketing.

If he's paying attention, he'll finally see that someone can love him without setting themselves on fire to keep him warm. Just living that truth beside him was its own curriculum, whether he liked the lesson or not.

Therapy is his only ticket out of economy-class avoidance and into anything resembling emotional business class. That is freedom.

Nothing motivates a man like him more than a spotlight with no shadows left to hide in. And unlike a conversation, he won't get defensive when he reads this, because a book isn't *me attacking him*. It's him encountering himself in a contained, safe space, without me standing there holding a flashlight under his chin.

He'll realize how deeply I understood him, and how little he had yet understood himself. And that is exactly where evolution begins.

What he's feared all along was never intimacy with me. It was intimacy with himself. This book is that bridge.

In the end, this may be the most loving thing I've ever given him: a way out, whether or not he ever walks back toward me.

I didn't write this book to save him. But if he returns to therapy and reads it with courage instead of defensiveness, he may finally understand what freedom, presence, and accountability actually feel like.

And that might change the entire trajectory of his life, which, between us, would be the plot twist of the century.

I did send him a couple of texts to encourage him to read his book.

Dear JJ,

I hope you read this book about you. It will give you insight into your dysfunction, patterns you can't name, behaviors that quietly sabotage you, and with therapy, I can say with confidence that you'll finally understand what absolute freedom feels like.

I wrote it primarily for my own healing and clarity, to understand your afflictions, because you are, undeniably, a fascinating and deeply instructive case study in psychology. But I also wrote it because I care about you and your mental well-being. Physical, emotional, and psychological health are all part of becoming a whole, happy, and well-adjusted person.

It hurts to watch you suffer like this. I understand that if you don't know anything different, you believe you're fine.

I tried to help you more than most people ever would, and that's how much I cared. But you have to want to help yourself, too. I hope that one day you can read this, laugh, learn, and maybe even sit with it as friends, knowing I was never angry with you, only honest, and always wishing you well.

And if nothing else lands, you'll at least get to marvel at how thoroughly one man managed to keep me on my toes without ever quite standing on his own.

Exhibit 68: The Archaeologist and the Ashes
The Woman Who Left the Museum and Locked the Door

By the time the dust settled, I realized I'd been both the exhibit and the archaeologist, the one on display and the one doing the digging.

What began as chemistry and curiosity slowly became a full-scale excavation project: decoding someone who couldn't even name his own patterns, let alone repair them. I kept thinking closure might surface in a conversation, at a dinner, in a text, or in an apology. Instead, I uncovered shards of inconsistency, emotional fragments with no map and no museum label.

Eventually, I understood something essential: friendship is nearly impossible now. Not because of anger, there is none, but because I illuminate his deepest dysfunction simply by existing in the same room. I'm not a friend to him; I'm a walking progress report.

The moment I enter, his system scrambles, as if I've arrived holding a clipboard and a truth-serum drip. It isn't that I'm too much; it's that his wiring can't tolerate being seen without reaching for the eject button.

How do you build any friendship with someone whose coping mechanisms hijack the moment you say hello? Until he can stand five minutes of sincerity without pulling a fire alarm, friendship remains a fantasy.

Ironically, Massi mentioned that JJ said I was egotistical.

JJ experiences me as "egotistical" not because I'm self-absorbed, but because I'm self-possessed. To someone who relies on avoidance and comfort to regulate himself, a woman who is independent, transparent, and emotionally intact feels confrontational by default.

My boundaries read as ego, my clarity reads as attack, and my refusal to bend or shrink to make him comfortable reads as superiority.

He was drawn to my strength as long as it was available to him — but the moment that same strength was applied to him, it exposed his limits. Calling me egotistical is simply the safest way for him to avoid confronting his own lack of capacity.

Months of bespoke dysfunction left me with a particular kind of relational hypervigilance, the kind that settles into your spine and quietly tracks the exits. After enough ghostings, reversals, and logistical acrobatics, my nervous system stopped believing in steadiness. So now, when men behave normally, text plainly, follow through, stay calm, cause no daily scheduling trauma, it almost feels suspicious.

What's your angle?
Why aren't you love-bombing or dodging?
Where's the ambient guilt? The spiritual bypass?

It's emotional jet lag. I've landed somewhere more peaceful, but my body still braces for turbulence.

Exhibit 69: The Reliability Breakdown

(a.k.a. The Accountability Sinkhole)

Location: West Wing of Emotional Infrastructure
Audio Guide Duration: 1 minute, 47 seconds (or the average time he can tolerate accountability)

Overview:
Witness how avoidant dysfunction transforms basic follow-through into an existential crisis. Visitors are advised to wear hard hats. Promises may collapse without warning.

Emotional Reliability: 0.5/10

When expectations rise, the specimen enters hibernation mode.
Texts vanish.
Birthdays evaporate.
Empathy drifts away like smoke.
His nervous system hears *reliability* and translates it as a *life sentence*.

Practical Reliability: 2/10

Returning keys = facing closure → mission aborted.
Confirming plans = implied commitment → system error.
Small proposed errands = emotional Mount Everest.
On rare successful missions, the subject requests praise, snacks, and a nap.

Accountability: 1/10

When confronted with impact, he deploys the **Deflection Trifecta™**:
- Reframe the offense ("That's just your perspective.")
- Intellectualize the wound ("We all interpret things differently.")
- Exit the scene before consequences load.

To the untrained eye, this can look manipulative.
To emotional anthropologists, it's shame-avoidance dressed as logic.

Interpretive Label:
He wants to be dependable. He doesn't want to feel depended on. The result is *Psychological Schrödinger's Boyfriend*: simultaneously caring and absent, responsible and unreachable.

Field Notes from the Curator:
I've carbon-dated this behavior before. The fossils always tell the same story: a man who mistakes showing up for surrender. With avoidants, reliability spoils faster than fresh ricotta; the moment you depend on them, they self-combust.

And then it finally clicked.

I wasn't asking for sainthood. I was asking for baseline adulthood, the kind that doesn't require subtitles or a legal disclaimer.

So, I stopped trying to fix the machinery and started documenting the malfunctions, displaying the artifacts of avoidance so I never have to live inside them again.

The museum is closed.
The door is locked.
And the archaeologist has gone home.

Closing Time at the Museum of Dysfunction

Because some ruins aren't meant to be restored.

Sometimes I picture myself standing outside that museum of dysfunction, holding a glass of champagne, finally free. I look at the building and think, *Oh God, I lived in there.* Then I laugh, because of course I did. We all live in some version of it at some point.

"Here we see the rare Florentine Jurassic Jackass, known for emotional hibernation, seasonal withdrawal, and chronic avoidance of accountability. Once believed extinct, this particular species reappears during moments of intimacy, stress, or dinner plans, only to vanish again when directly asked how he feels."

The backdrop was Florence.
The special effect was one profoundly under-evolved man.

I walked away from him not because the tether snapped or the universe announced the lesson complete, but because loving him required a level of emotional self-abandonment I refuse to practice anymore. His ice storms, disappearances, and Battistero-cold silences were quietly eroding parts of me I had spent years reclaiming.

The inconvenient truth no memoirist wants to admit is this: sometimes the story doesn't end just because you end it. Sometimes the tether still hums.

Even after I folded the chapter shut, life and he refused to stay inside the lines I drew. He reappeared in long hugs that lasted one beat too long. In quiet eye contact, everything it revealed was meant to be hidden. Then, out of nowhere, in five words I never expected from an avoidant dinosaur:

"Portami un piccolo pensiero." Please bring me a small thought.

A token.

A tether.

A sanctioned way to remember me.

I didn't realize at first that what he meant was, "*Choose something of you that I'm allowed to keep.*"

So maybe the story isn't, *I walked away and never looked back.* Maybe it's this: I walked away with my self-respect intact, and the tether remained, light as a thread, quiet as breath—the kind of connection that exists between two people who are never ready at the same time.

Whatever this was, it never belonged to a tidy genre.

Still, I got my ending, because I finally chose myself, even if the tether between us glows faintly in the dark.

You don't walk through something like this and come out believing your own fantasies anymore. The woman who fell for his potential was operating on hope. The woman standing here now runs on data, boundaries, and a wicked sense of humor.

That evolution didn't happen because of him. It happened despite him.

It happened because I refused to stay trapped in his spiral. I walked myself out, one hard truth at a time, one small, painful realization after another.

Healing is when you finally admit they were selling potential, not reality.

Closure isn't a hug. It's the decision to stop applying for building permits in a fault line area.

So, I kept walking.

Because the museum closes at 7 p.m., and I have dinner plans with someone who's actually alive.

No crystals.
No disappearing acts.
He shows up on time.
Texts when he says he will.
And returns my keys.

Because in this museum, the only exhibit I'm curating now is peace.

Welcome to the Museum Gift Shop (Archive)

The exhibition has ended.

The following pages are preserved at *JurassicJackass.com* as a separate archival insert for readers who wish to continue. They are not part of the main collection and require no emotional investment.

Think of this as after-hours access.

Proceed only if you enjoy satire, artifacts, and proof that healing doesn't erase humor — it just relocates it.

Originally rendered in color.